ABC Reading eggs

My First Spelling

By Sara Leman

Ages 5–7

Dear Parent or Carer,

This book is part of the **My First** series of **Reading Eggs** workbooks. **Reading Eggs** has proven to be very popular with parents, children and teachers. The **Reading Eggs** books and website have helped more than 20 million children worldwide learn to read.

Each vibrant book in the **My First** series includes a wide range of interesting activities that will help your child develop essential reading and writing skills. Written by experienced teachers and educators, the series supports what your child learns at school.

The pages are clear and uncluttered, with activities that build real skills. Activities are fun and motivate children to continue working and learning. Instructions are easy to follow and regular challenges entice children to extend their learning.

I hope that you and your child enjoy using this and other books in the series.

Kind regards, *Katy Pike*
Publisher

ABC Reading Eggs My First Spelling

ISBN: 978-1-74215-164-9

Reprinted 2012, 2013, 2014, 2015, 2016, 2019, 2020, 2021, 2022, 2023, 2024, 2025

Distributed by:
Pascal Press
PO Box 250
Glebe NSW 2037

www.readingeggs.com
Written by Sara Leman
Publisher: Katy Pike
Editors: Amanda Santamaria and Stacey Weston
Design and layout by Modern Art Production Group
Printed in China by 1010 Printing International Ltd

Contents

Spelling activities		4
Sound chart		6
Lessons 1 – 5	Short **a** words	8
Lessons 6 – 7	Short **e** words	18
Lesson 8	Plurals	22
Fun spot 1		**24**
Lessons 9 – 12	Short **i** words	26
Lessons 13 – 15	Short **o** words	34
Lesson 16	Plurals	40
Fun spot 2		**42**
Lessons 17 – 20	Short **u** words	44
Lesson 21	Plurals	52
Fun spot 3		**54**
Lessons 22 – 27	Blends	56
Lessons 28 – 29	**oo** words	68
Lesson 30	**ump** words	72
Lesson 31	Plurals	74
Lesson 32	Words with **er**	76
Fun spot 4		**78**
Certificate		80

Spelling activities to do at home

- Save old magazines and junk mail. Use them for a variety of activities including:
  - searching for and circling particular words, such as **the**, **it**, **and**
  - identifying one-, two-, three- or four-letter words etc.
  - cutting out individual letters or words to create a collage
  - cutting out pictures for your child to label.

- Allow your child to play with magnetic letters on the fridge to create words. Rearrange the letters to make new words, e.g. tops = pots, stop.

  Create crosswords, e.g.

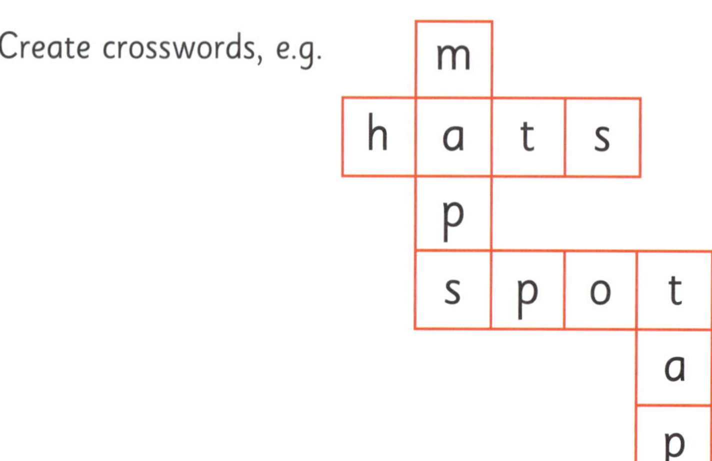

- Help your child to make the association between spelling and meaning. Encourage them to write their name and create simple labels for things. Let them see you writing a shopping list, a message or an email.

- Provide your child with a variety of writing and drawing materials. Encourage them to create their own cards and to write the messages inside. Let them practise addressing envelopes and provide them with a toy mail box so that they can 'post' their cards and letters.

- Spend time talking with your child and scribe their ideas as they speak. This enables you to model spelling conventions and reinforces for your child the link between spelling and meaning.

- Encourage your child to write letters or words on steamed-up mirrors and windows at home and in the car.
- Trace letters and words on your child's back and ask them to guess what you have written. Alternatively, ask your child to trace letters and words in the air with their finger.
- Allow your child to create letters or words in shaving foam, sand, paint, playdough, string or pavement chalk.

- Write a large letter on a piece of paper and ask your child to fill it with as many words as they can think of that start with that letter.
- Play games such as 'I spy something beginning with ...' and 'I spy something that rhymes with ...'
- Play a variation of hangman. Choose a word that the child knows and ask them to fill in the blanks. Alternatively play 'What am I writing?' Write the first letter of the word and ask your child to guess what the word might be. Then write the second letter and so on until your child guesses correctly or the word is complete.
- Use the **Reading Eggs Alphabet flashcards** and the **Reading Eggs Beginning to Read flashcards** to practise making new words. Activities to try include:

Reading Eggs Alphabet flashcards

- **Game 3** Sound Hunt
- **Game 7** Making Words

Reading Eggs Beginning to Read flashcards

- **Game 1** Letters and Sounds
- **Game 2** Blends and Digraphs
- **Game 3** Rhyming Words
- **Game 5** Make a Sentence

Sound chart

Short vowels

Short vowel sounds

a as in **a**pple

e as in **e**lephant

i as in **i**gloo

o as in **o**range

u as in **u**mbrella

Long vowels

Long vowel sounds

a as in **a**p**e**

e as in b**ee**

i as in p**ie**

o as in r**o**p**e**

u as in c**u**b**e**

Digraphs

ch as in
Charlie **Ch**imp

sh as in
Shelly **Sh**ark

th as in
Thingamabob

Long vowel sounds and spellings

Sound	Common spelling	Alternative spelling			
ai	rain	**a** - baby	**a_e** - cave	**ay** - day	**ey** - prey
ee	knee	**ea** - eat	**e** - he	**ey** - key	**ie** - piece
igh	light	**ie** - pie	**i_e** - like	**uy** - buy	**y** - sky
oa	boat	**o** - so	**oe** - toe	**o_e** - mole	**ow** - mow
ue	glue	**ew** - chew	**oo** - boot	**u_e** - rule	

Lesson 1 • at

Wordlist sat mat cat bat fat hat
rat a at it flat that

1 Label each picture.

c______

b______

h______

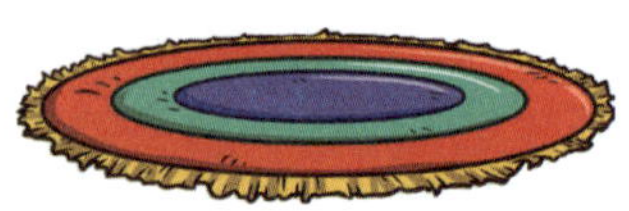

m______

r______

f______

2 Find the words.

3 Write the hat words in alphabetical order.

________ ________ ________

4 Complete the words. Use Ding Bat's letters.

fla____

t____at

____t

____at

____at

____t

t h
c i
a f

CHALLENGE Unjumble these words.

tfla ________ htta ________

Lesson 2 • ap, am

Wordlist tap map cap nap jam ram
ham am as has clap swam

1 Trace and write.

ap ______

am ______

2 Write each word.

t______

m______

c______

j______

r______

n______

3 Write each word family.

nap
ham
cap
jam
tap
am

ap

am

4 Unjumble the jigsaw. Write the words.

CHALLENGE

Write sentences using these words.

clap swam has

Lesson 3 • ad

Wordlist sad mad bad dad pad lad pads
an and had glad add

1 Write the **ad** words. Join one word to each picture.

s________

d________

l________

p________

2 Find the words.

3 **Circle the ad words.**

Ladbug was sad. His dad was mad with him. This had been a bad day!

Colour in a pad each time you find an ad word.

4 **Trace.**

Complete the sentence.

an glad had dad

Dan is __________ . His __________ __________ got him __________ ice-cream.

spda ____________ dda ____________

Lesson 4 • ag, an

Wordlist bag sag rag fan ran tan
man the to in flag than

1 **Make a word on the fridge with each letter.**

Trace.

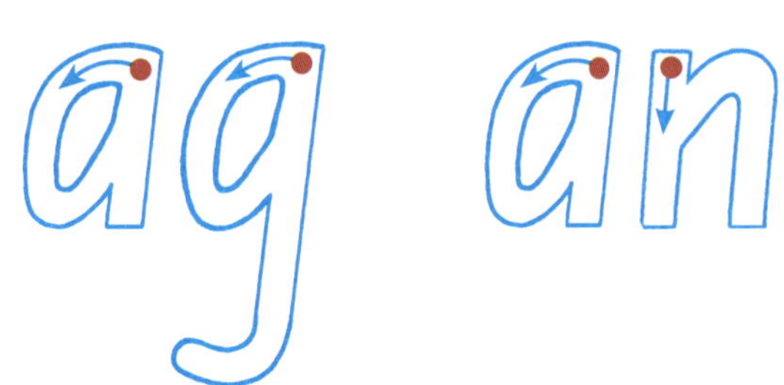

2 **Write these words in alphabetical order.**

3 Crack the code!

t = ✿
h = ✚
e = ★
o = ▲
i = ✓
n = ✷
a = ♥
m = ■

1 ✿ ✚ ★ ______

2 ✿ ♥ ✷ ______

3 ✿ ▲ ______

4 ■ ♥ ✷ ______

5 ✓ ✷ ______

6 ✿ ✚ ♥ ✷ ______

4 Write a sentence using Sandy Can's word.

flag

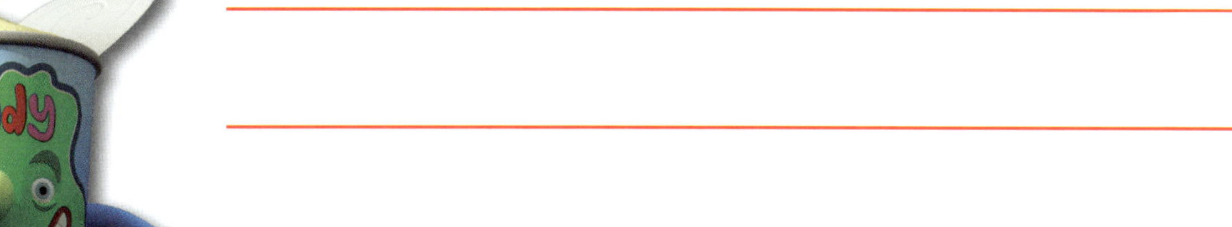

CHALLENGE Circle the hidden words.

a b a g e f a n l m a n f t h e z t h a n w

Lesson 5 • as, ab

Wordlist as has gas grab cab lab
crab no me is able table

1 Colour the ab words.

2 Unjumble the jigsaw. Write the words.

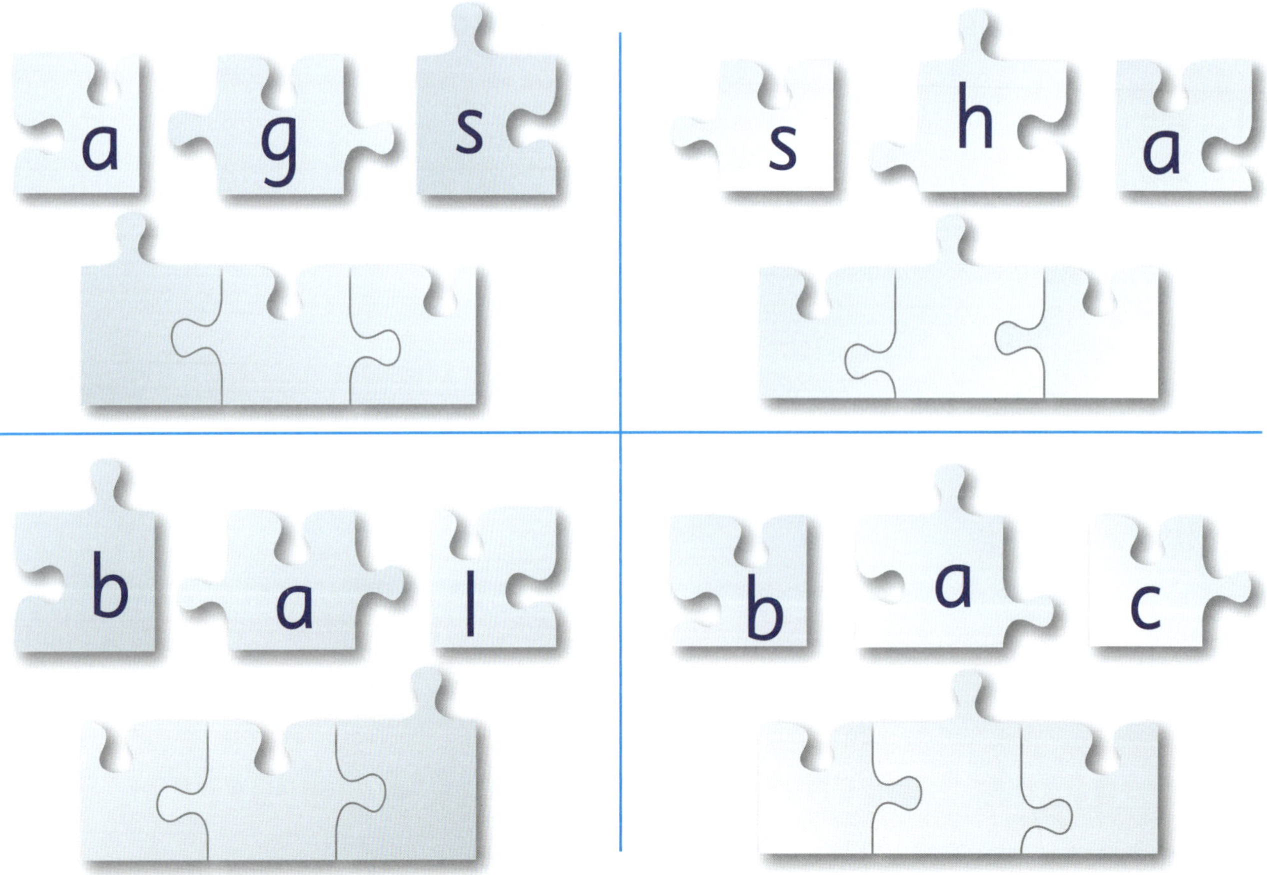

a g s

s h a

b a l

b a c

3 Read the clue to finish the word.

I have a hard shell.
I am a ____ab.

A scientist works here. I am a ____ab.

I can take you somewhere.
I am a ____ab.

You can eat your meals here.
I am a __________.

4 Guess the word by its shape. Write each word in a box.

able table no grab

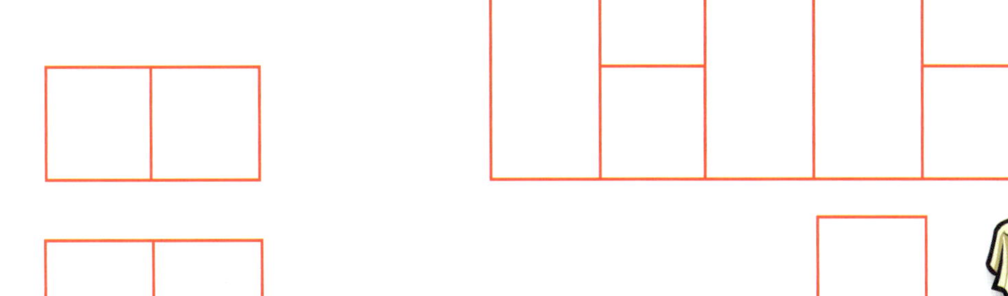

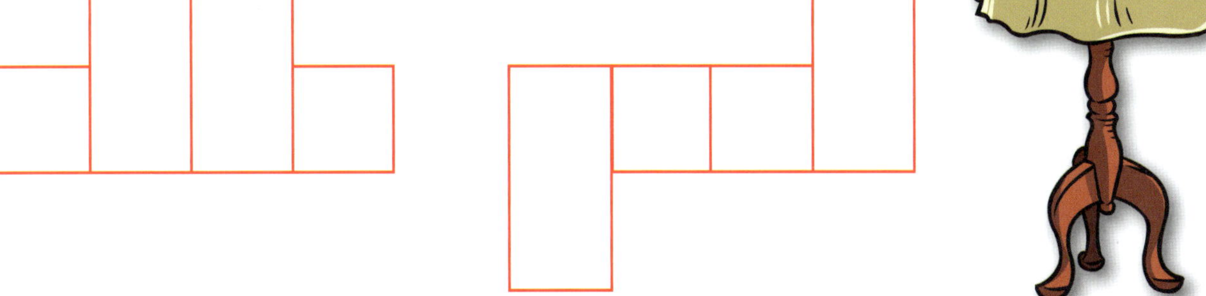

CHALLENGE

Write a rhyming word from your list for each word.

be go cable

Lesson 6 • ed, eg

Wordlist bed fed red wed peg beg legs my he go shed egg

1 **Draw.**

a red bed

an egg with legs

2 **Colour ed words red. Colour eg words green. Write them.**

3 Find the words. Colour: my = blue, he = red, go = green.

m	y	h	e	g	o
g	o	m	y	h	e
h	e	g	o	m	y
m	y	h	e	g	o
g	o	m	y	h	e
m	y	g	o	h	e

4 Circle the correct word. Cross out the wrong word.

Peggy Leg has a big beg bed .

Red Rabbit has long legs eggs .

Go Go Gizmo has a wed shed .

CHALLENGE Unjumble these words.

dhse ____________ selg ____________

Lesson 7 • en, et

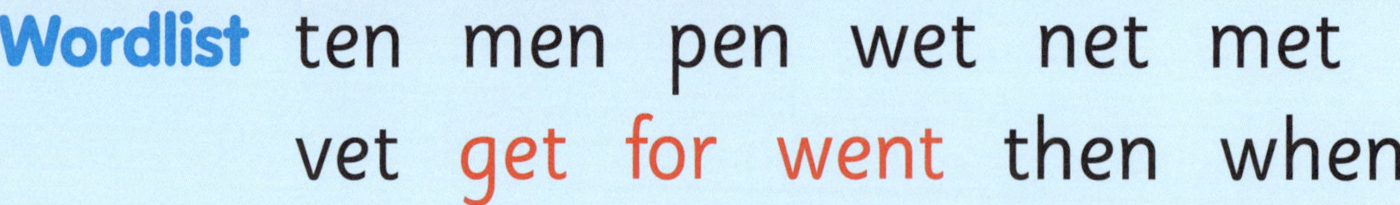

Wordlist ten men pen wet net met
vet get for went then when

1 Write the words. Join one word to each picture.

m ______

v ______

n ______

p ______

2 Write each word family.

ten wet met pen net men

en	et

3 Follow the string. Write each word you make.

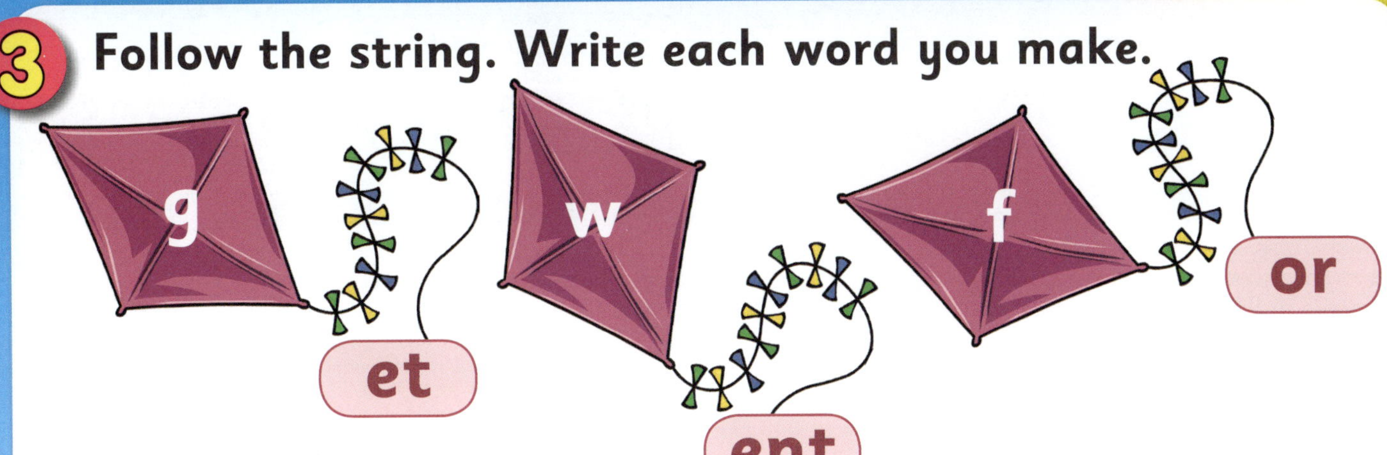

4 Trace.

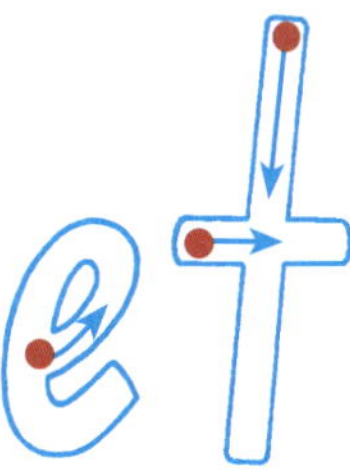

Complete the sentences.

pen When went

________ can I see Jet Set?

Zen Ten ________ to the park.

Big Ben needs my ________ .

CHALLENGE

Write sentences using these words.

then met get

Lesson 8 • More than one

Wordlist mats cats maps bags pets hens beds we if of crabs sheds

1 For these words add s to make the plural, eg one ant, two ants.

mat
cat
map
hen
bag
bed

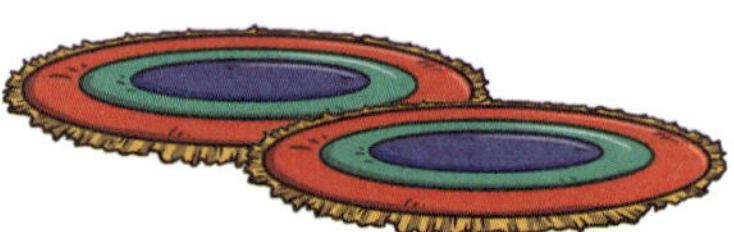

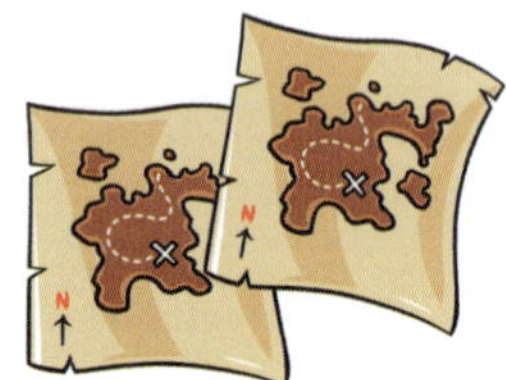

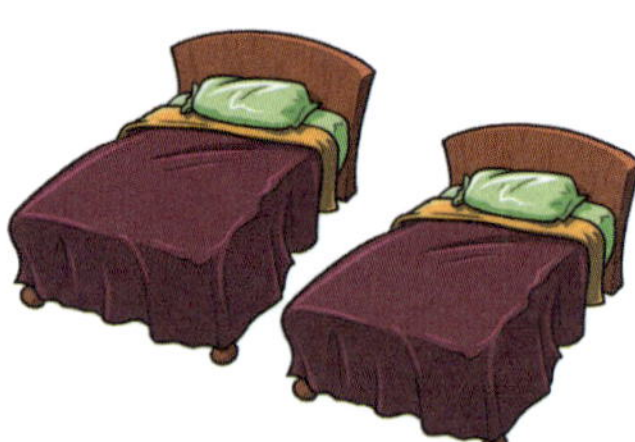

2 Colour the plural words.

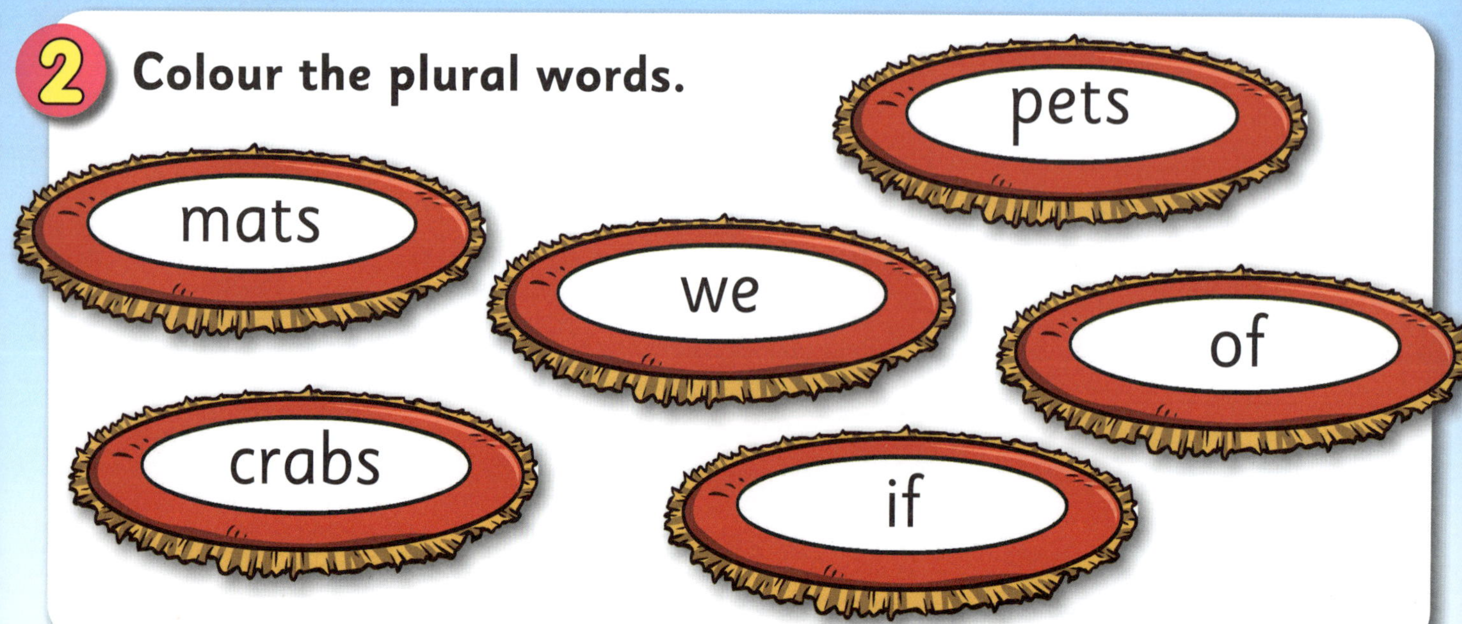

3 Write these words in alphabetical order.

pets

bags

______________ ______________ ______________

4 Help Tom the Dog get back to his kennel. Draw a track of words that are correct.

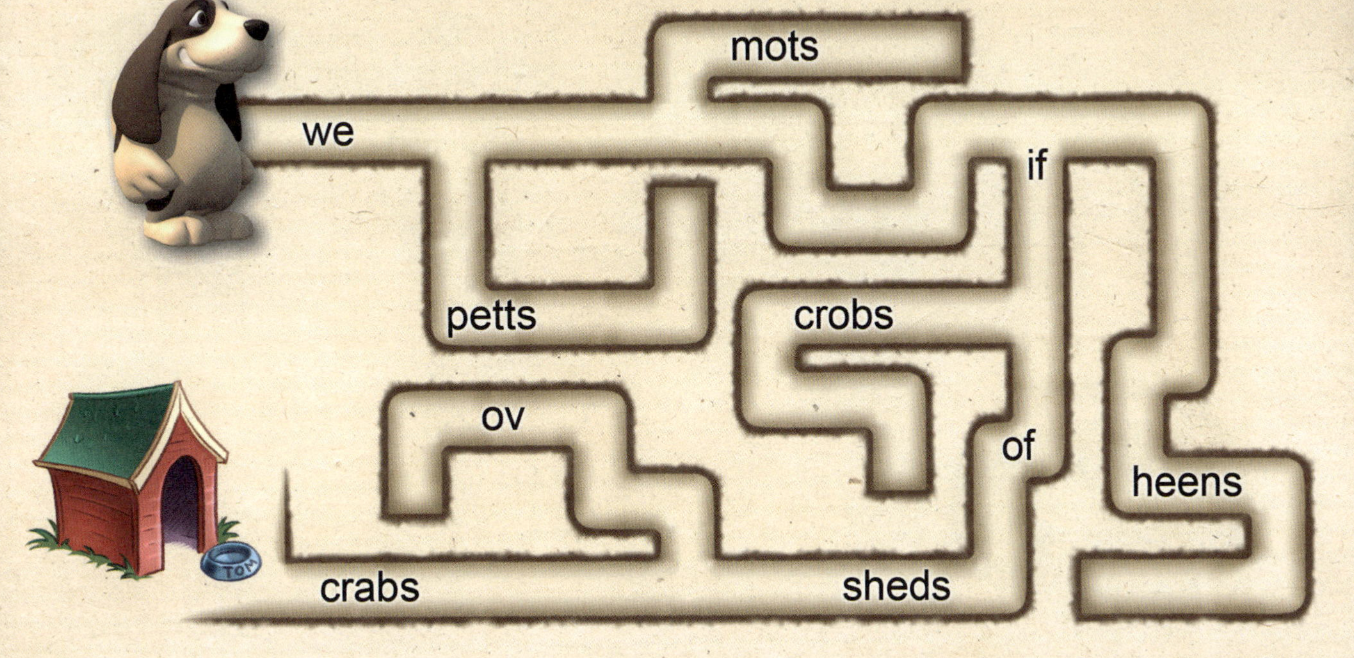

CHALLENGE Circle the hidden words.

o m a t s e m a p s s p e t s w e s h e d s

Fun spot 1

1 **Complete the crossword. Use the picture clues to help you.**

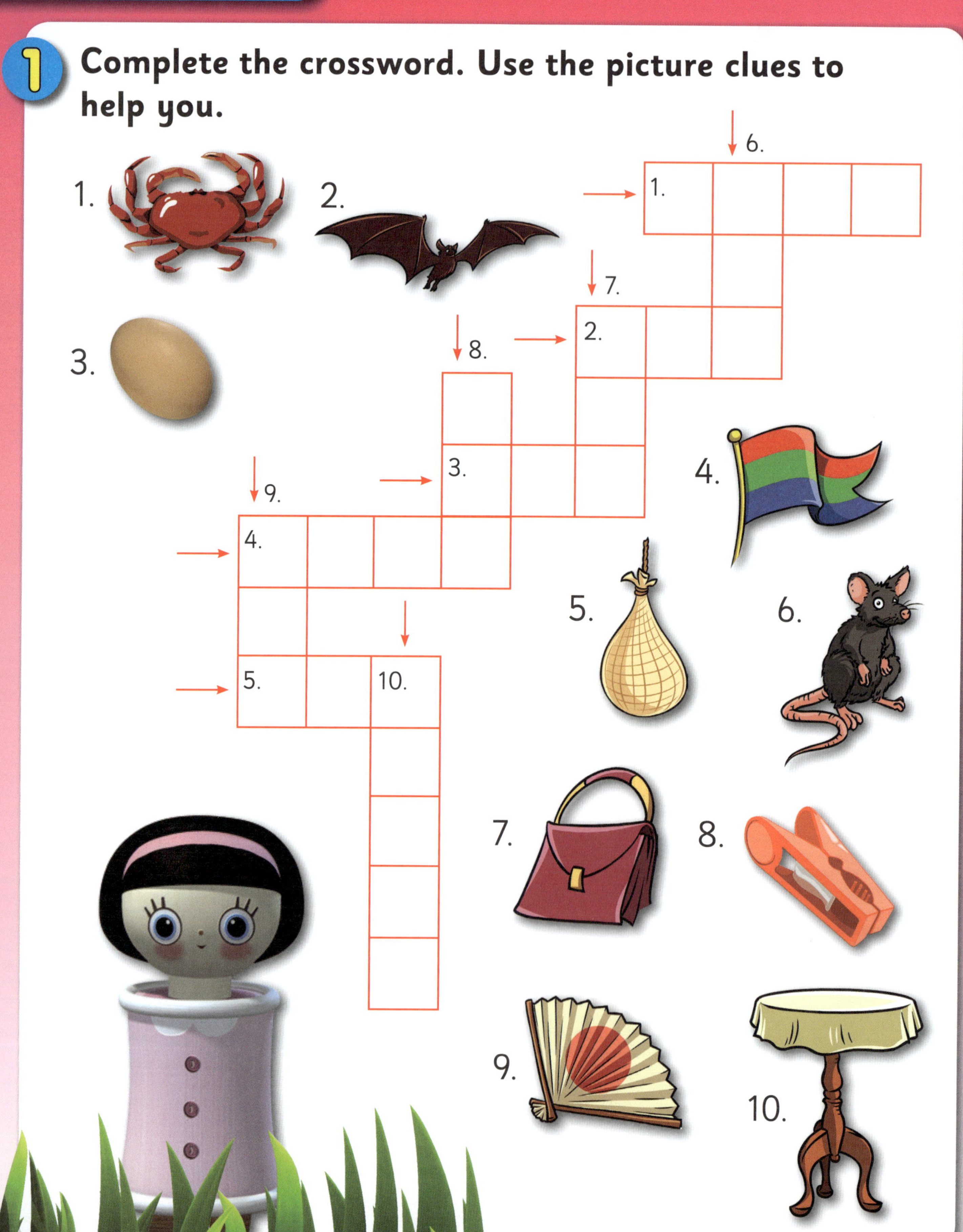

2 Join the pictures to the word family. Write the word.

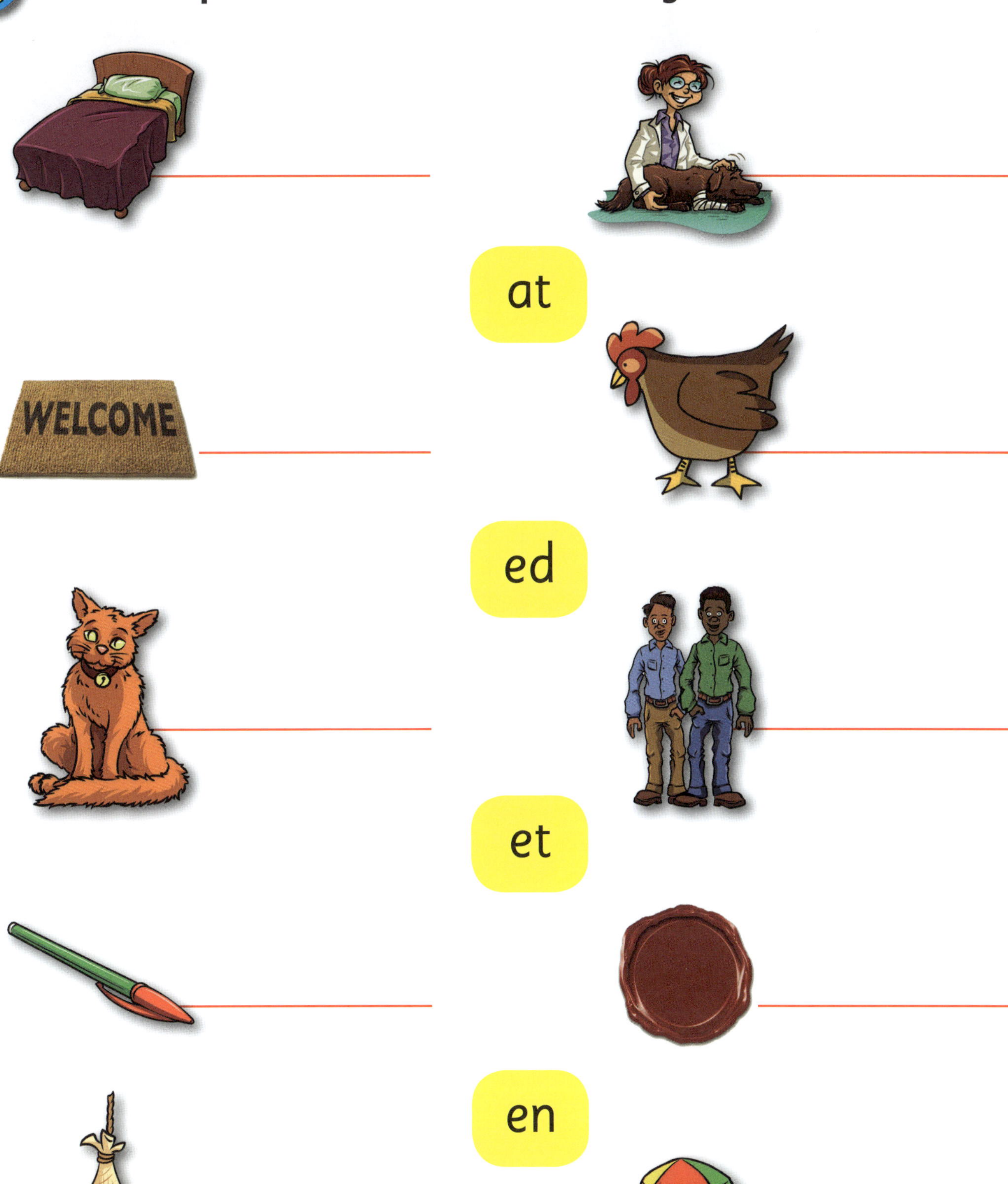

Lesson 9 • ig

big pig rig wig dig fig jig
his him you twig wigs

1 Draw.

a wig on Big Pig

a fig on a twig

2 Label each picture.

p

b

j

f

d

w

3 Crack the code!

s = ✿
i = ✚
m = ★
h = ▲
u = ✓
o = ✹
y = ♥
g = ■
w = ◆
r = ●

1 ▲ ✚ ★

______

2 ◆ ✚ ■

______

3 ♥ ✹ ✓

______

4 ● ✓ ■ ✿

______

5 ▲ ✚ ✿

______

6 ● ✚ ■

______

4 Write a sentence using Big Pig's word.

dig

______

______

______

______

CHALLENGE

Write sentences using these words.

wig his jig

Lesson 10 • id, it

Wordlist kid hid lid did bit sit hit
it they she grit fits

1 Trace.

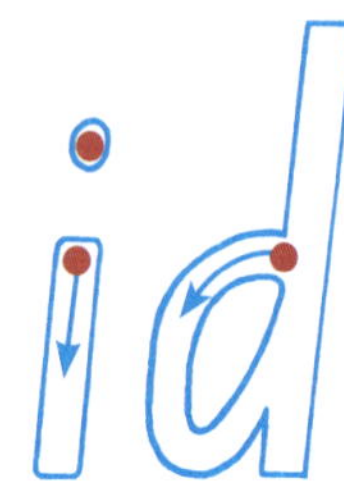

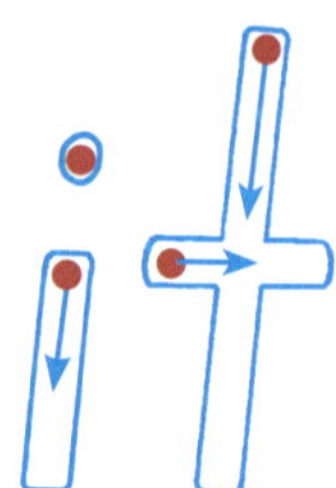

Colour the id words blue. Colour the it words red.

kid	it	did	lid	sit
hid	grit	bit	fits	hit

2 Find the words.

3 Complete the words. Use Sid the Kid's letters.

sh____

the____

l____d

bi____

hi____

4 Complete the sentences.

Kid She They

________ are Icy Mice.

________ is Meg the Hen.

This is Sid the ________ .

CHALLENGE Write a rhyming word from your list for each word.

bid __________ kit __________

me __________ hay __________

Lesson 11 • in, ip

Wordlist bin tin pin win tip sip rip
said that all drip hint

1 Label each picture. Use the words.

bin
win
sip
rip
pin
tin

2 Write the words in the correct tin.

tip win drip
pin rip bin

3 Follow the critters to the food. Write each word.

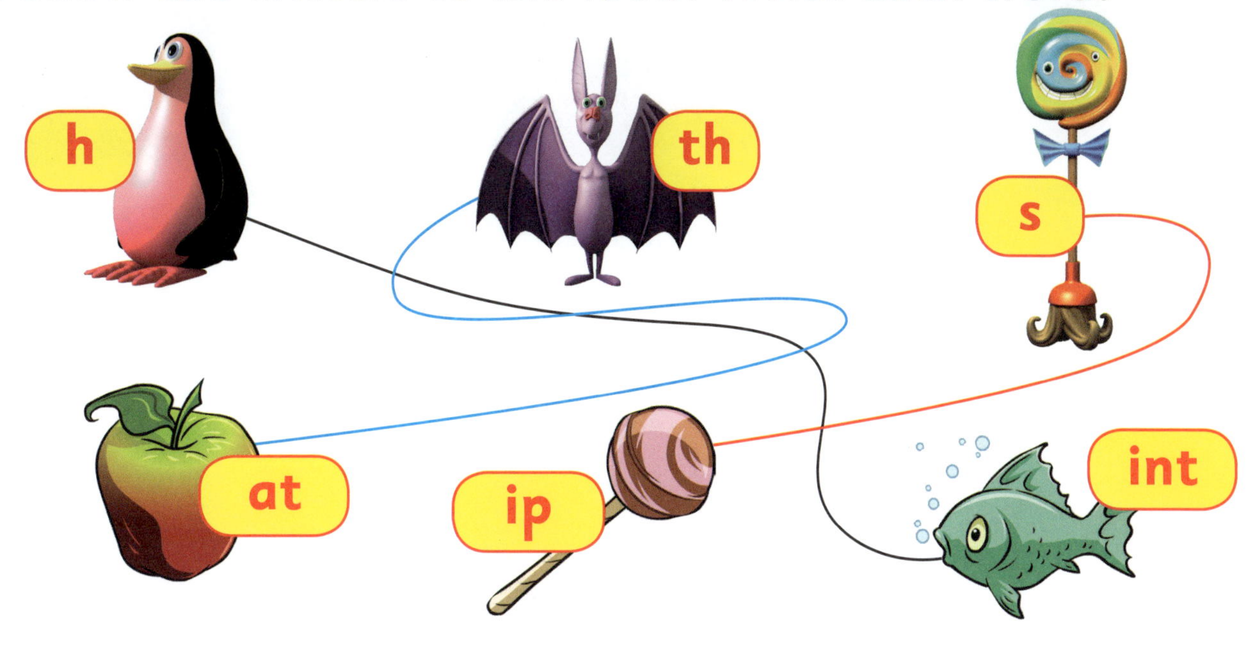

______________ ______________ ______________

4 Circle the correct word. Cross out the wrong word.

Pinkipoo sed said she was happy.

We can all awl see Flobby.

Gus can tipp tip out the rubbish.

CHALLENGE Unjumble these words.

dsia ______________ tihn ______________

Lesson 12 • ix, ax

Wordlist fix six mix mixer tax fax wax
with are her axe sixty

1 Write the words. Join one word to each picture.

m________

w________

s________

a________

2 Make a word on the fridge with each letter.

s

m

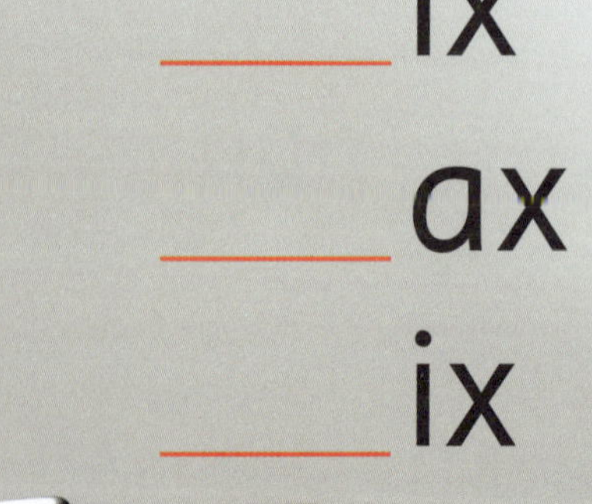

_____ix

_____ax

_____ix

_____ax

3 Unjumble the jigsaw. Write the words.

4 Guess the word by its shape. Write each word in a box.

her mixer sixty with wax

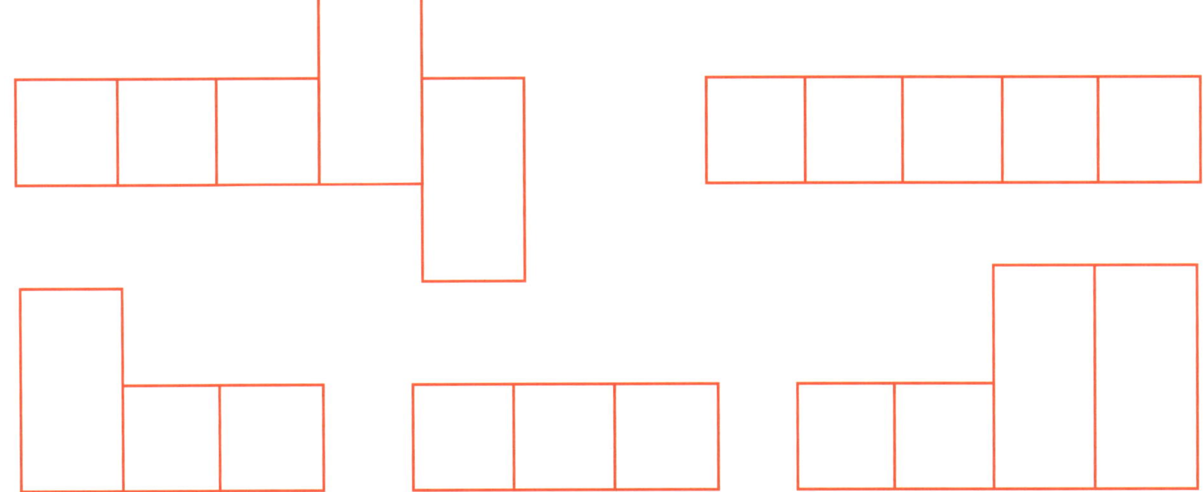

CHALLENGE

Write sentences using these words.

sixty mix fax

Lesson 13 • ob, og

Wordlist rob job sob dog bog fog logs
what out on frog trod

1 **Trace.**

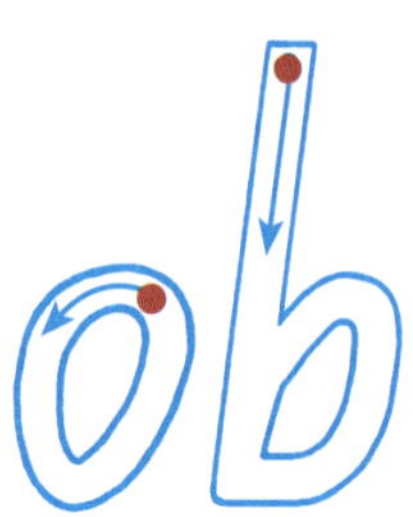

og

Draw.

a dog in the fog

a frog on some logs

2 **Colour ob words red. Colour og words green. Write them.**

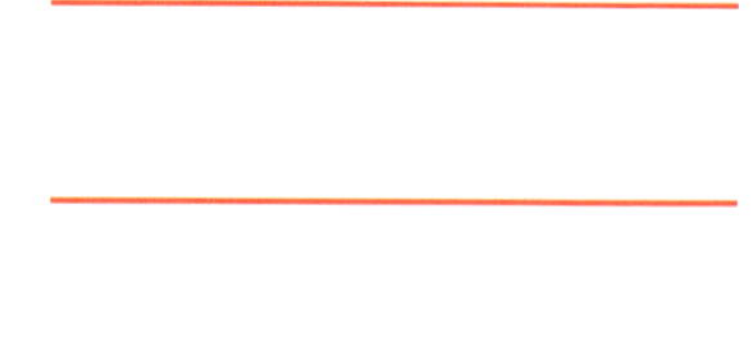

3 Write the words in alphabetical order.

4 Help Wobble Blob get back to the jelly. Draw a track of words that are correct.

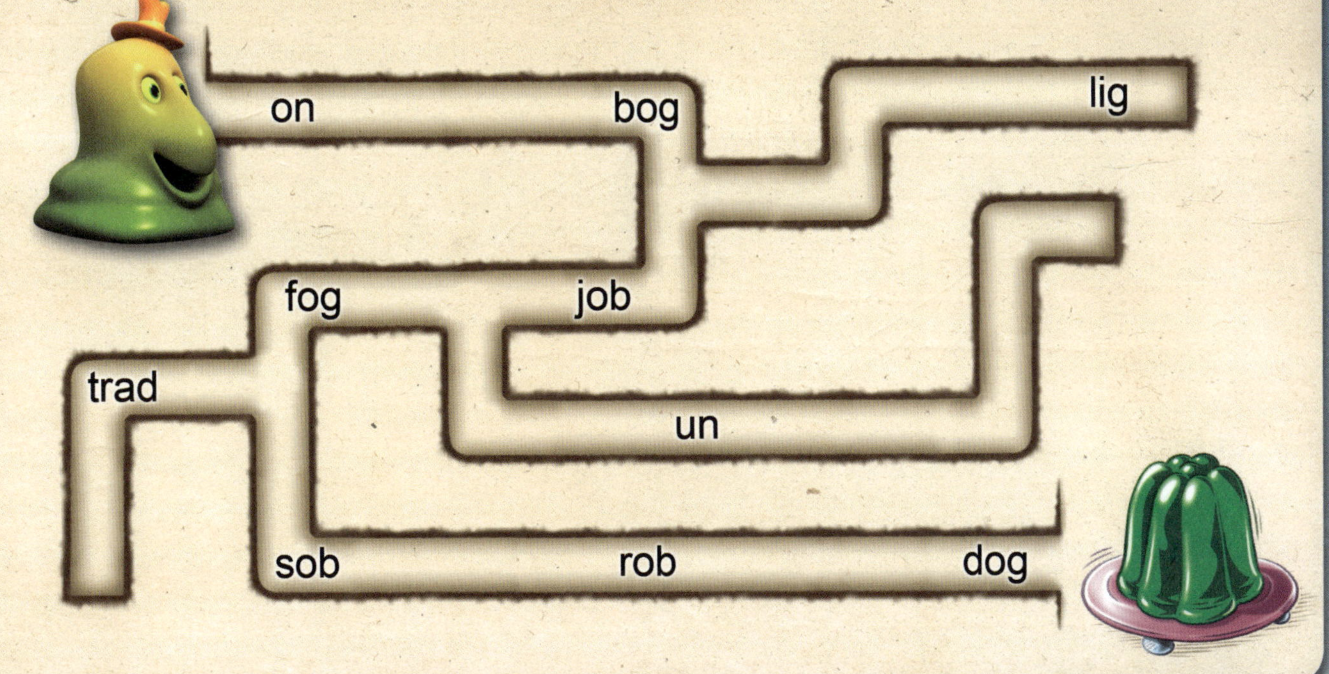

CHALLENGE Circle the hidden words.

yrobxbogtfogllogs

Lesson 14 • ox, op

Wordlist box fox top cop hop mop pop
there this have chop stop

1 Colour the op words.

cop
hop
top
mop
pop

2 Write the words in the correct box.

box chop fox stop
hop cop pop

3 Complete the words. Use Socky Fox's letters.

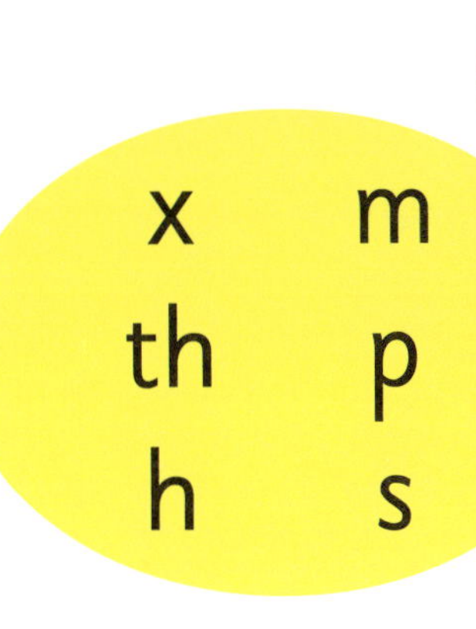

thi____

____ave

____ere

bo____

ho____

____op

4 Complete the sentences.

stop hop Mop

Lollipop ________ cleans the floor.

Sixty Six has to ________ .

Kangako likes to ________ .

CHALLENGE

Find the words in your list that mean the same as:

burst slice peak own

Lesson 15 • od, ot

Wordlist cod nod pod rod cot pot hot
come some not spot dotty

1 Label each picture.

2 Colour od words blue. Colour ot words red. Write them.

nod not pot
cod spot pod

3 Crack the code!

t = ✿
o = ✚
n = ♦
m = ★
s = ✓
e = ✸
c = ♥

1 

____

2 ♦ ✚ ✿

____

3 ♥ ✚ ★ ✸

____

4 Write a sentence using Dotty Sun Spot's word.

hot

____

____

____

____

Write a rhyming word from your list for each word.

potty rot mum odd

Lesson 16 • More than one

Wordlist lids hits pots wigs lips hips frogs but be like boxes ships

1 Add s to make the plural, eg one bed, two beds.

lid
lip
pot
wig
ship
frog

______

______

______

______

______

______

2 Colour the plural words.

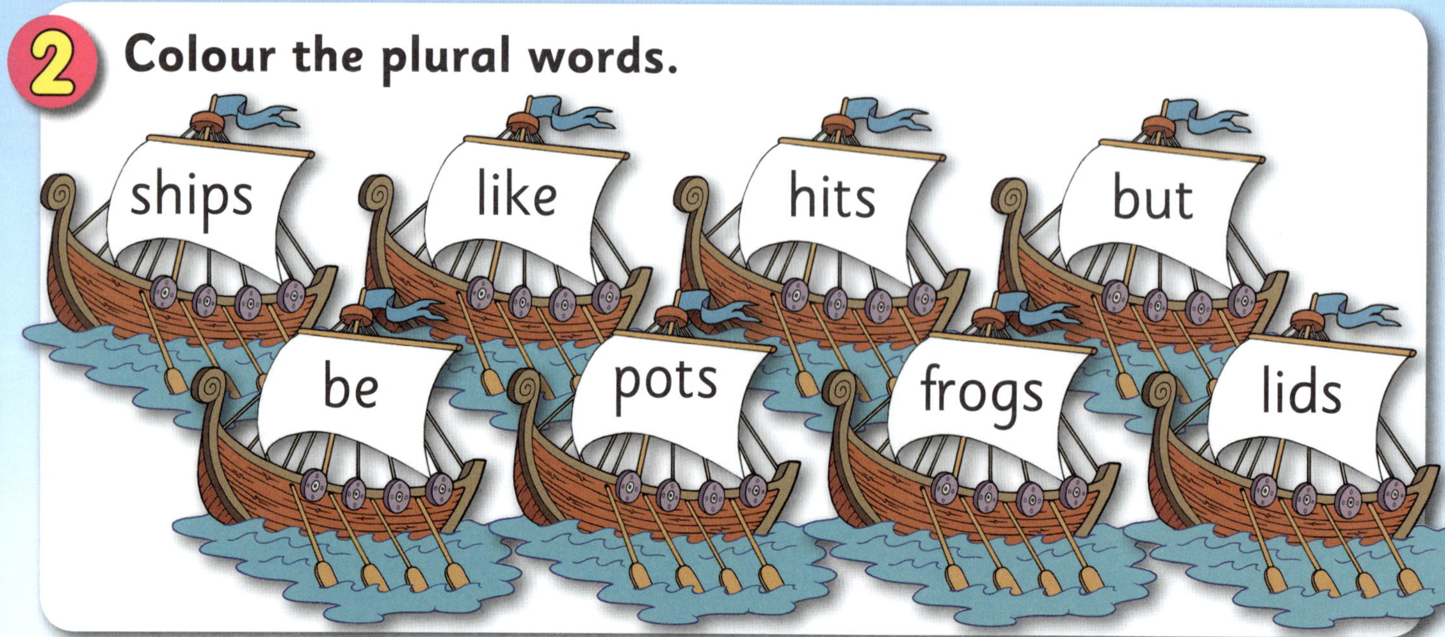

3 Read the clue to write the word.

You can kiss with me.

I am ________.

We are made of cardboard.

We are ________.

We live in a pond.

We are ________.

We are big boats.

We are ________.

4 Complete the crossword.

1. 

2. 

3. 

4. 

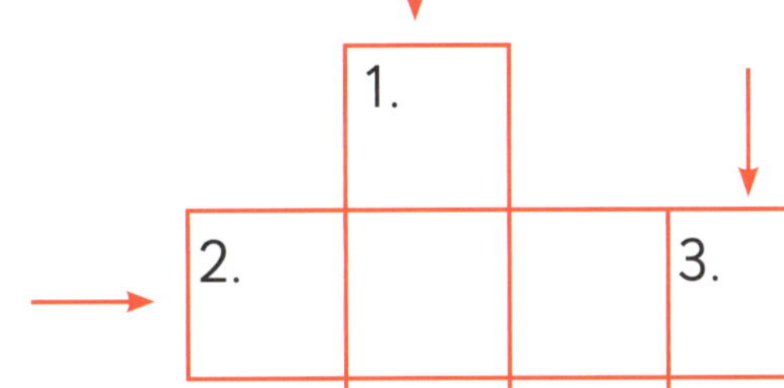

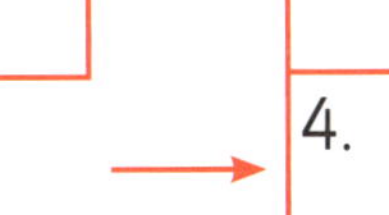

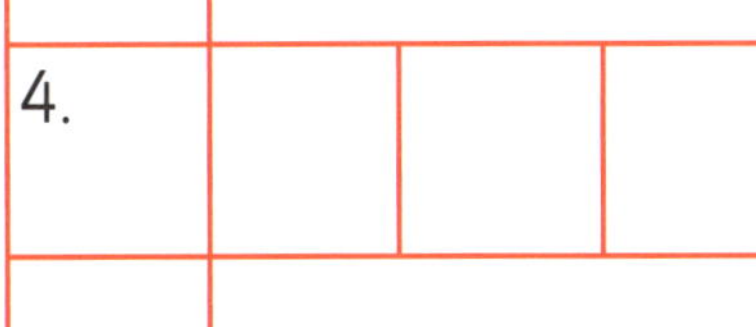

CHALLENGE

Write sentences using these words.

boxes lids ships

Fun spot 2

1 Find the words. Colour: wig orange, pot pink, box blue, job red, hit green, pin yellow.

w	i	g	h	i	t	j	o	b	p	i	n
b	o	x	p	o	t	p	i	n	w	i	g
h	i	t	j	o	b	w	i	g	b	o	x
p	o	t	p	i	n	b	o	x	h	i	t
j	o	b	w	i	g	h	i	t	p	o	t
p	i	n	b	o	x	p	o	t	j	o	b
w	i	g	h	i	t	j	o	b	p	i	n
b	o	x	p	o	t	p	i	n	w	i	g
h	i	t	j	o	b	w	i	g	b	o	x
p	o	t	p	i	n	b	o	x	h	i	t
j	o	b	w	i	g	h	i	t	p	o	t

2 Power words. Join the letters to make the word.

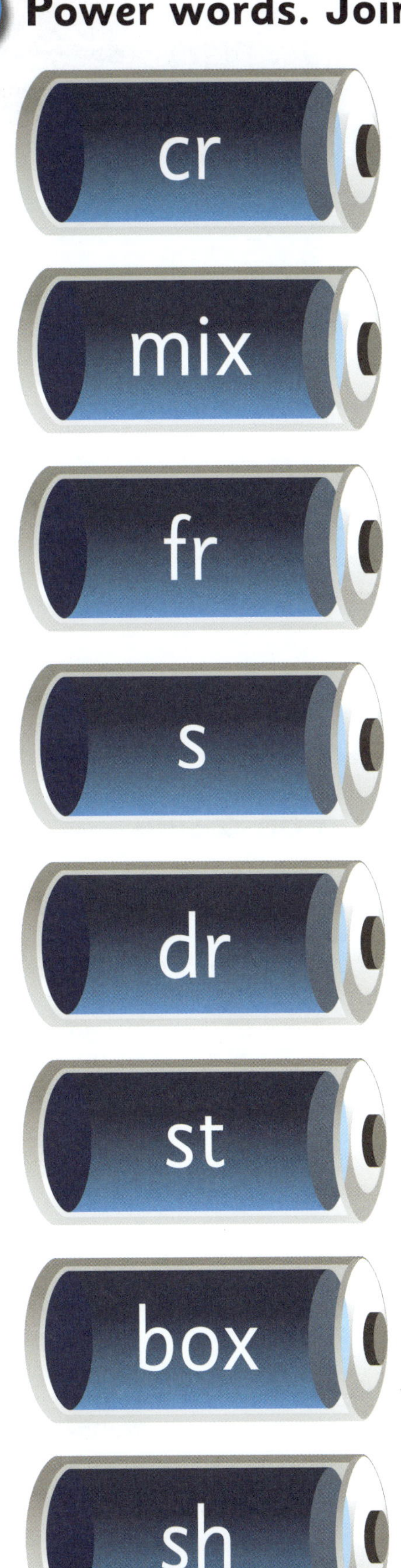

Lesson 17 • ug

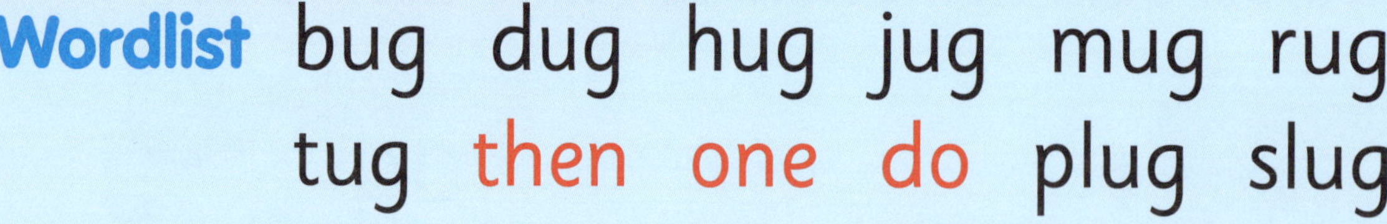

Wordlist bug dug hug jug mug rug
tug then one do plug slug

1 Draw.

a jug on a rug

a bug on a slug

2 Label each picture.

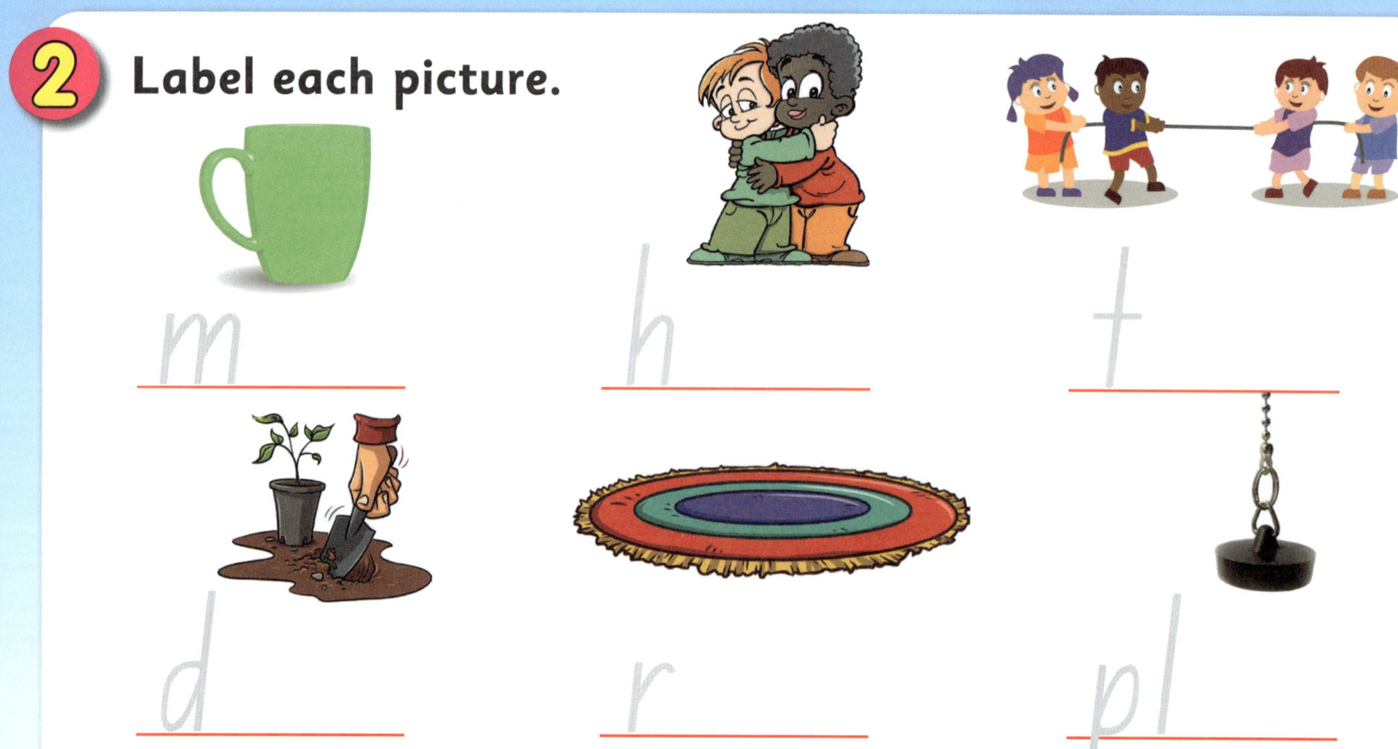

m______ h______ t______

d______ r______ pl______

3 Follow the chain. Write each word.

______ ______ ______

4 Complete the sentences.

Do one Bug

Say hello to Tug Boat ______.

______ you like Ladbug?

Zee Wee only has ______ eye.

CHALLENGE Circle the hidden words.

y t u g g m u g l d o r s l u g t h e n x

Lesson 18 • um, ut

Wordlist gum hum sum but nut cut put
were them me drum bump

1 Write the words. Join one word to each picture.

s ______

dr ______

n ______

c ______

2 Colour um words red. Colour ut words blue. Write them.

______

______

______

______

______

______

3 **Guess the word by its shape. Write each word in a box.**

were them me bump

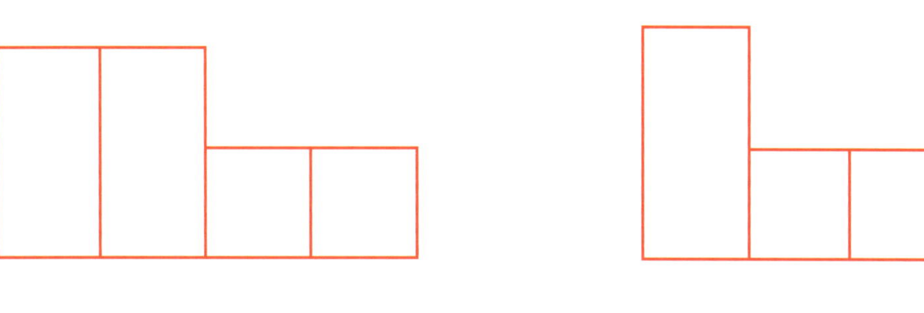

4 **Help Gutter Mutt find the nut. Draw a track of words that are correct.**

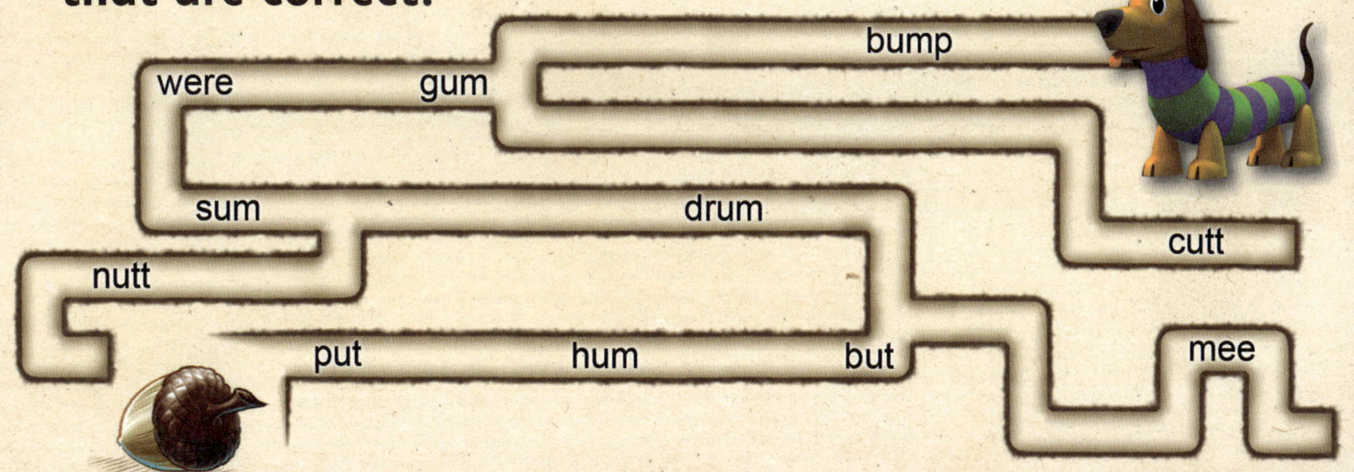

CHALLENGE Unjumble these words.

mbpu ____________ rwee ____________

Lesson 19 • un, ud

Wordlist bun fun run sun nun bud mud
down dad when thud hung

1 Label each picture.

b

n

m

b

s

r

2 Write the words on the correct bun.

fun mud run bud bun nun hung thud

un

ud

3 Complete the words. Use Dotty Sun Spot's letters.

mu___

whe___

hun___

___un

b___d

d___d

n b
d u
a g

4 Write a sentence using Underting's word.

down

CHALLENGE

Find the words in your list that mean the same as:

cake muck jog father

Lesson 20 • up, us, ub

Wordlist pup cup bus cub tub rub club
up see come grub dust

1 Trace and copy each word.

2 Colour up words red. Colour us words blue.
Colour ub words green. Write.

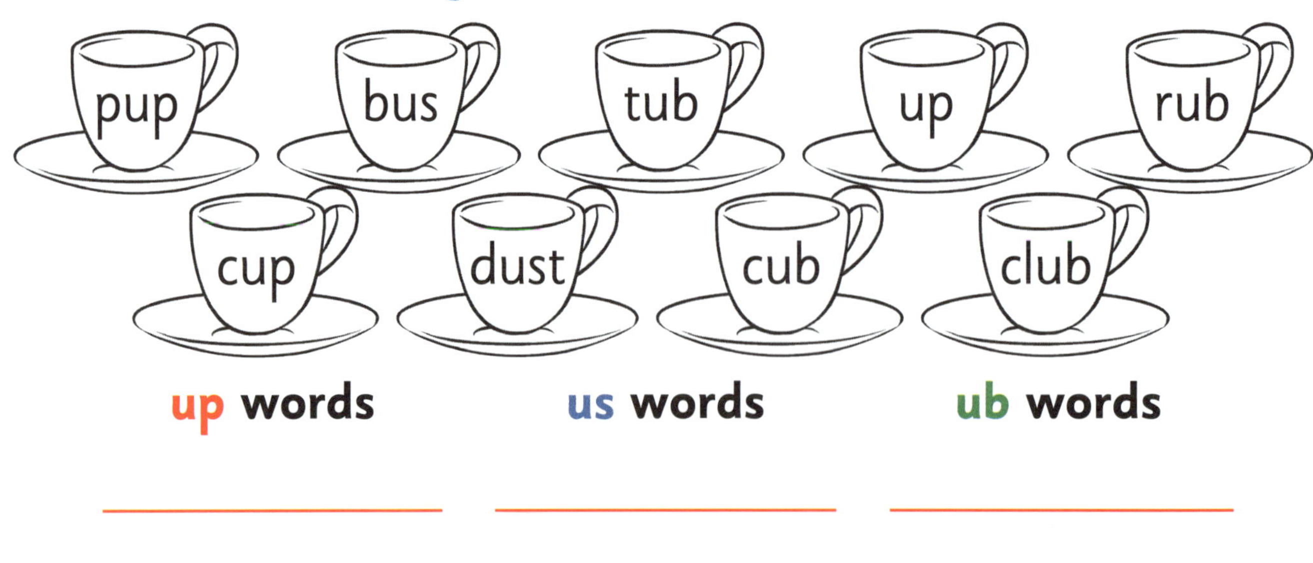

up words | us words | ub words

3 Write the words in alphabetical order.

______ ______ ______

4 Circle the correct word. Cross out the wrong word.

Gus is always full of dost dust .

Giddy Up plays with a pup pop .

Bubble Blow sits on a bas bus .

CHALLENGE

Write a rhyming word from your list for each word.

up scrub must some

Lesson 21 • More than one

Wordlist mugs rods dots tugs nuts suns
drums will into from buses spots

1 Add s to make the plural, eg one spot, two spots.

nut
mug
sun
rod
drum
dot

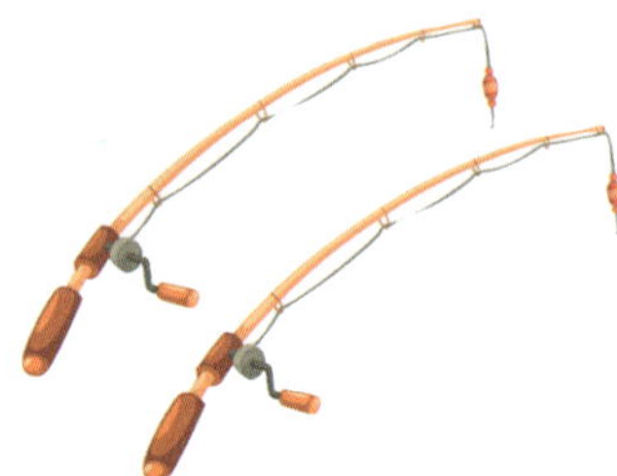

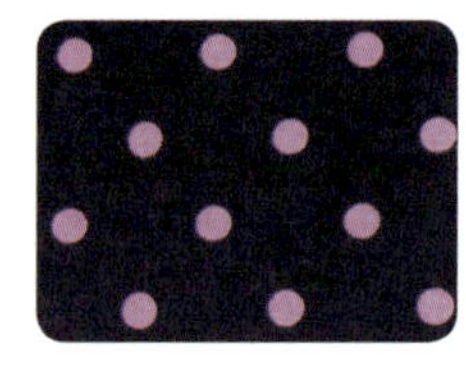

2 Colour the plural words.

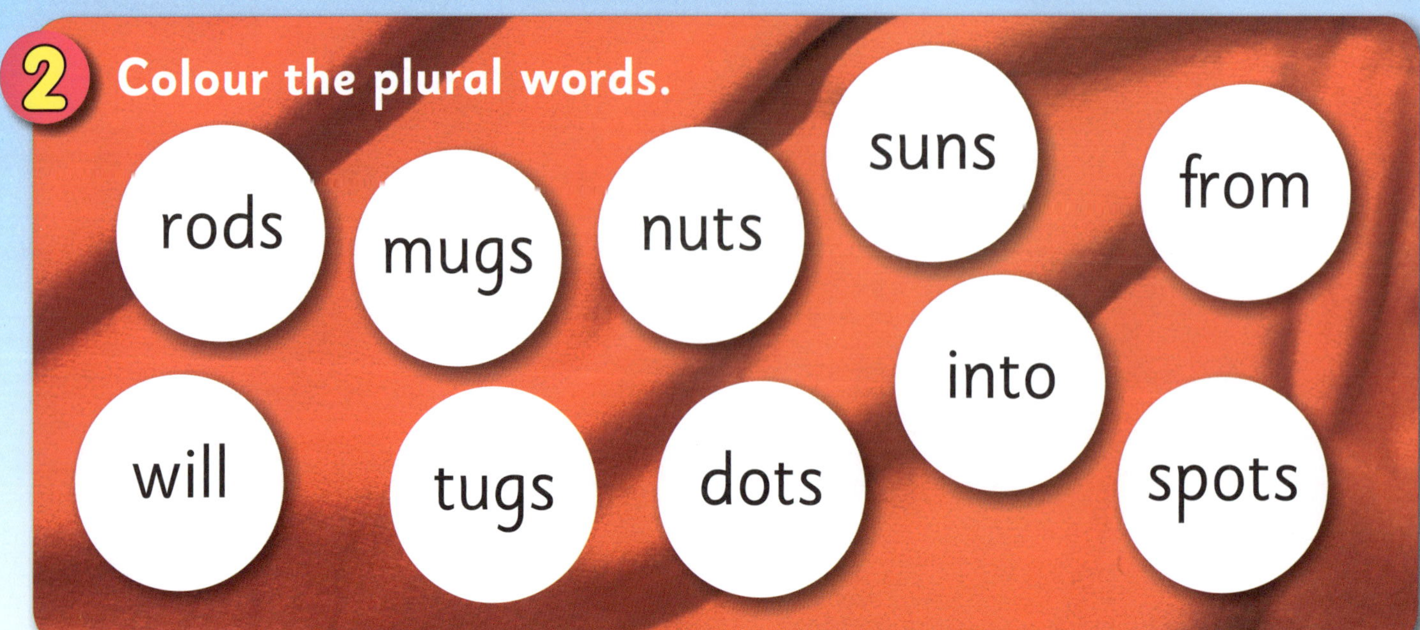

3 Crack the code!

Code
b = ✿
e = ★
u = ✚
s = ▲
m = ♥
g = ✓
t = ✸
n = ●

1 ✸ ✚ ✓ ▲ ______

2 ▲ ✚ ● ▲ ______

3 ✿ ✚ ▲ ★ ▲ ______

4 ● ✚ ✸ ▲ ______

5 ♥ ✚ ✓ ▲ ______

6 ✿ ✚ ✓ ▲ ______

4 Complete the sentences.

into spots drums

Dotty is a sun with ______.

Charlie can play the ______.

Jump ______ the sandbox.

CHALLENGE

Write sentences using these words.

buses mugs will

Fun spot 3

Make words using these letters.

t a h

2 letter word

3 letter word

u b s

2 letter word

3 letter word

n a l p

2 letter word

4 letter word

2 Join the pairs that rhyme. Write the words.

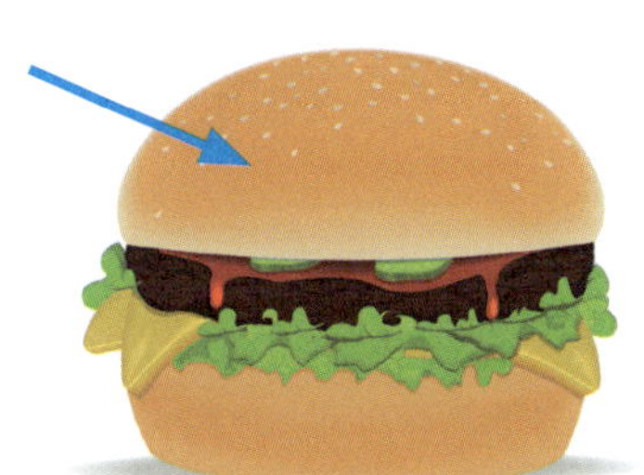

Lesson 22 • pl

Wordlist plan plot plop plum plus plug plant she play get pluck plump

1 Use the letters to make words.

pl

____ot
____ump
____ug

____an
____op
____us

2 Pull the plums apart to make words.

3 Find the words.

Colour: play = blue, she = red, get = green.

p	l	a	y	s	h	e
g	e	t	p	l	a	y
p	l	a	y	g	e	t
s	h	e	p	l	a	y
g	e	t	p	l	a	y

4 Complete the crossword.

1. 

2. 

3. 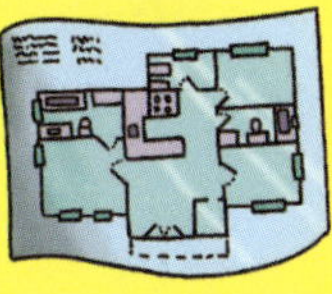

4. 

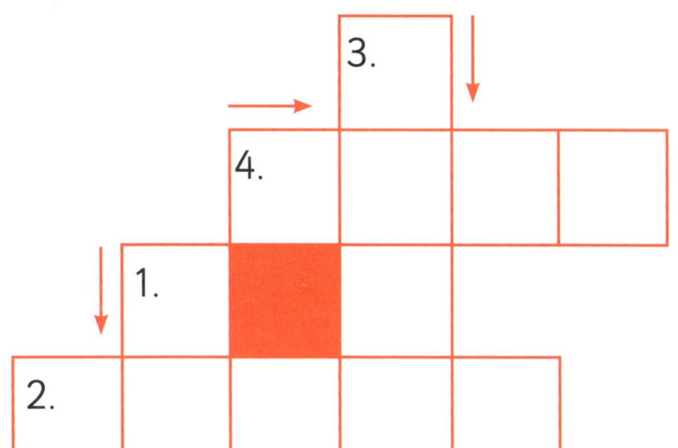

CHALLENGE Circle the hidden words.

sshebplopnplugmgetcpluck

Lesson 23 • sk

Wordlist skip skin skid disk risk tusk ask just now came skunk skill

1 Join the jigsaw pieces to make words. Write them.

2 Colour the words that contain sk.

3 Read the clue to write the word.

You can do this with a rope.

____

I am on the outside of your body.
I am _______________.

I have fur and I am very smelly!

____

Elephants have two of me.
I am a _______________.

4 Guess the word by its shape. Write each word in a box.

skin came skill disk ask

CHALLENGE Unjumble these words.

ustj _______________ ikrs _______________

Lesson 24 • ck

Wordlist back neck sick duck rock lock muck got their your clock stick

1 Label each picture.

b

n

s

d

r

cl

2 Draw.

a duck on the pig

Scribble Stick with a clock

3 Complete the words. Use Fluff the Duck's letters.

____ock

go____

m____ck

thei____

____uck

____our

4 Circle the correct word. Cross out the wrong word.

Tick Tock Clok Clock tells the time.

Gemma Giraffe has a long neck nek .

Gus the Dump Truck likes muk muck .

CHALLENGE

Write sentences using these words.

your sick lock

Lesson 25 • ft, lt

Wordlist gift left lift soft belt bolt melt could house too salt raft

1 Trace and copy each word.

bolt

2 Write the words on the correct gift.

gift soft
bolt lift
left belt
melt raft
salt

_ft

_lt

3 Follow the ribbon. Write each word you make.

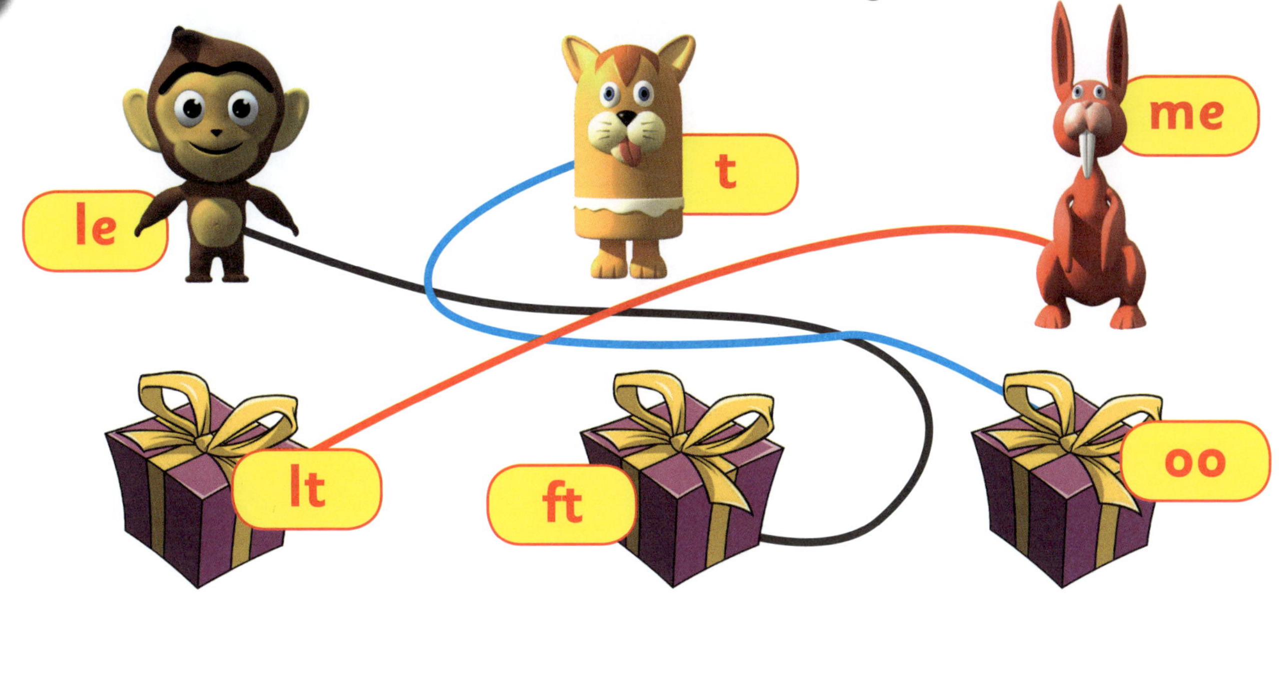

______ ______ ______

4 Complete the sentences.

house could raft

Octo Puss has a ride on a ______.
Sunny Snail has a shell for a ______.
Pinkipoo wishes that she ______ fly.

CHALLENGE
Find the words in your list that mean the opposite of:
hard freeze right drop

Lesson 26 • amp, ent

Wordlist camp damp lamp went sent bent tent was old by spent stamp

1 **Write the words. Join one word to each picture.**

2 **Colour amp words red. Colour ent words blue. Write them.**

3 **Unjumble the jigsaw. Write the words.**

4 **Help Flutter Bye Bye find the flower. Draw a track of words that are correct.**

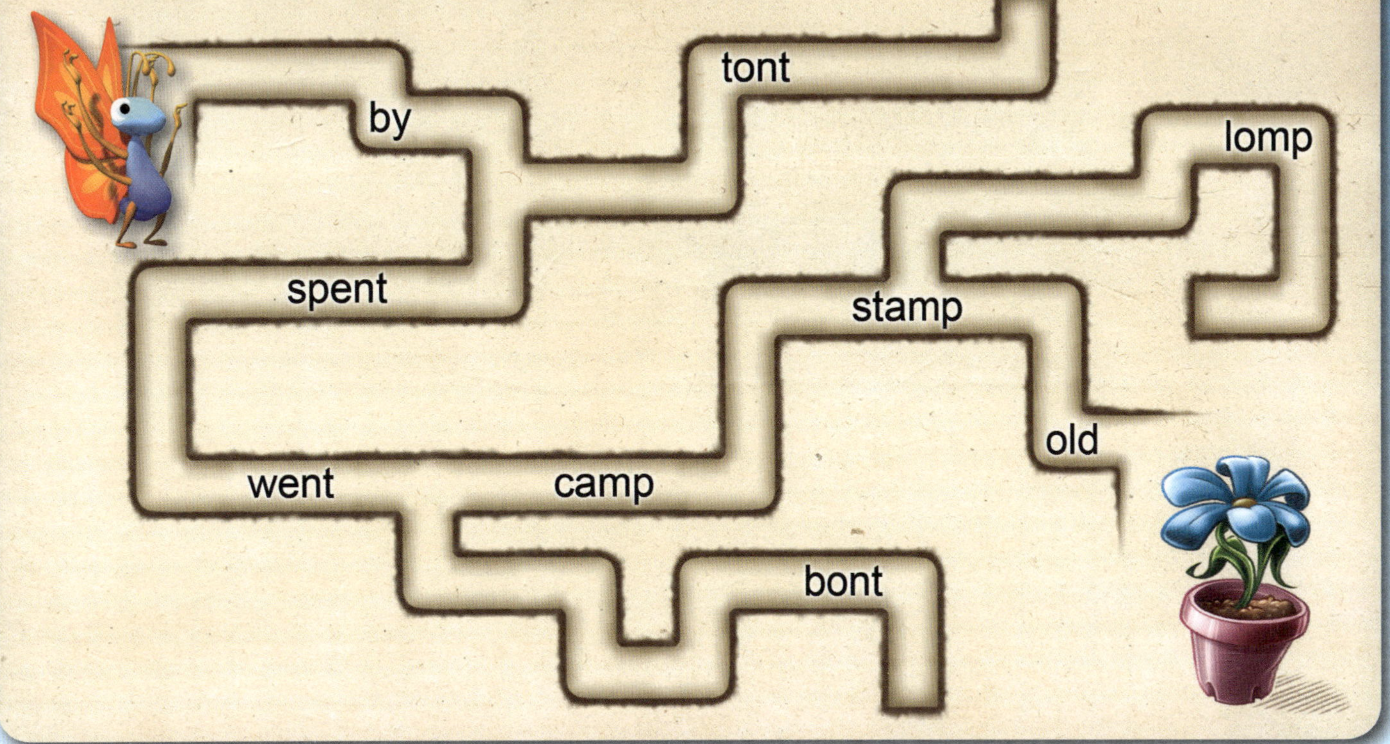

CHALLENGE

Write a rhyming word from your list for each word.

ramp rent my fold

Lesson 27 • ill

Wordlist bill fill will pill hill mill chill day made make until pillow

1 **Join each sound to the word machine.**
Write each word you make.

2 **Write the words in alphabetical order.**

3 Crack the code!

l = ■
y = ✿
e = ★
d = ✚
a = ▲
m = ♥
k = ✓
i = ✸

1 ♥ ▲ ✚ ★ ______

2 ♥ ▲ ✿ ______

3 ✚ ▲ ✿ ______

4 ♥ ✸ ■ ■ ______

5 ♥ ▲ ✓ ★ ______

6 ♥ ✿ ______

4 Circle the correct word. Cross out the wrong word.

Pram Lamb has a soft pilow pillow .

Wait until unitll Happy Nap is asleep.

Icy Mice will catch a chil chill .

CHALLENGE Circle the hidden words.

emaketpillefillnmade

Lesson 28 • ook, ool

Wordlist book cook took look hook pool cool time shine away school shook

1 Colour the ook words.

book took time hook

away cook look shook

2 Draw.

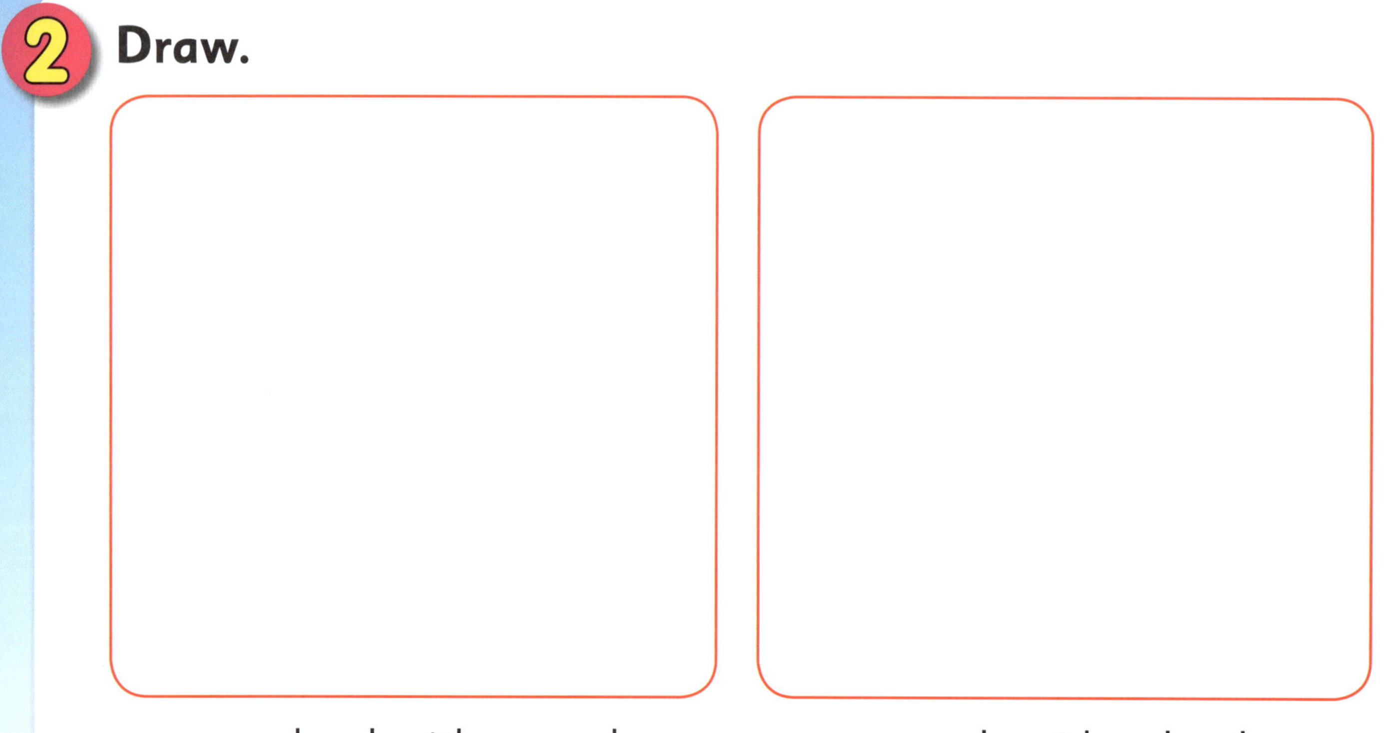

a school with a pool

a cook with a book

3 Underline the ool words.

Red Rooster loves his school.

It is cool. It has a big pool.

Colour a stool each time you find an ool word.

4 Guess the word by its shape. Write each word in a box.

shook shine away time

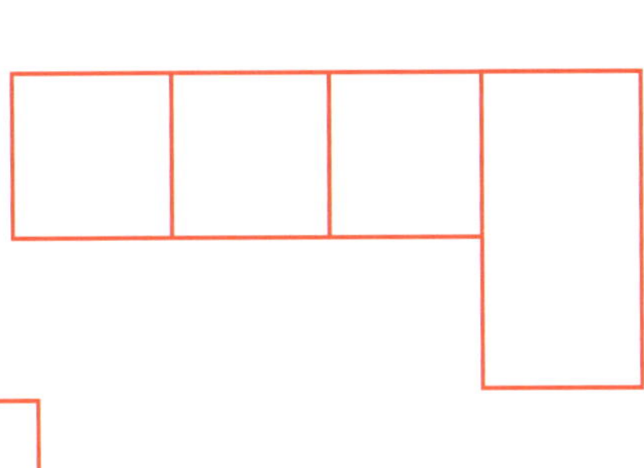

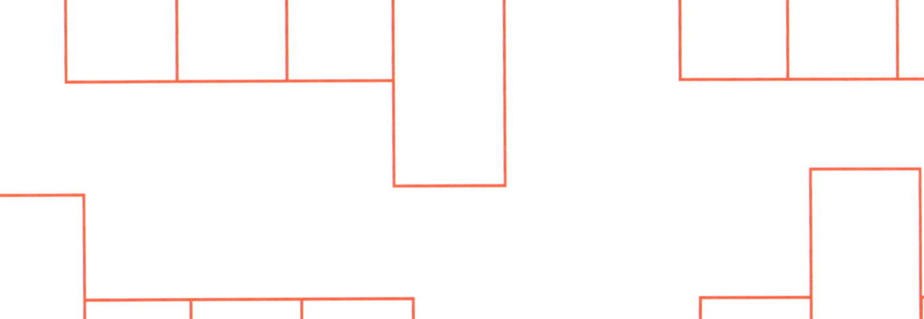

CHALLENGE

Write sentences using these words.

shook shine time

Lesson 29 • oot, oom

Wordlist boot hoot loot root foot room zoom called here off broom shoot

1 Write the words. Join one to each picture.

br________

f________

b________

r________

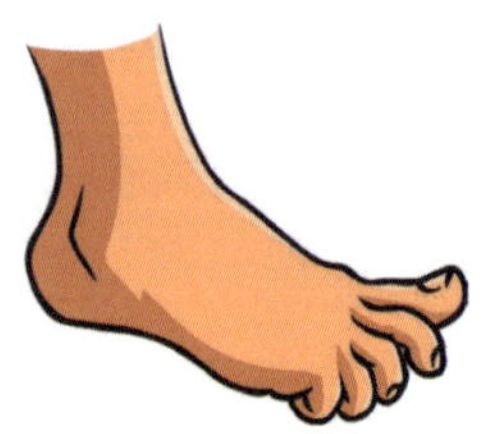

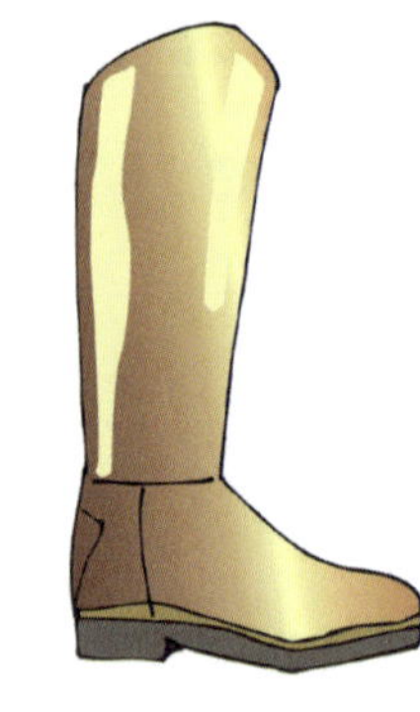

2 Find the words.

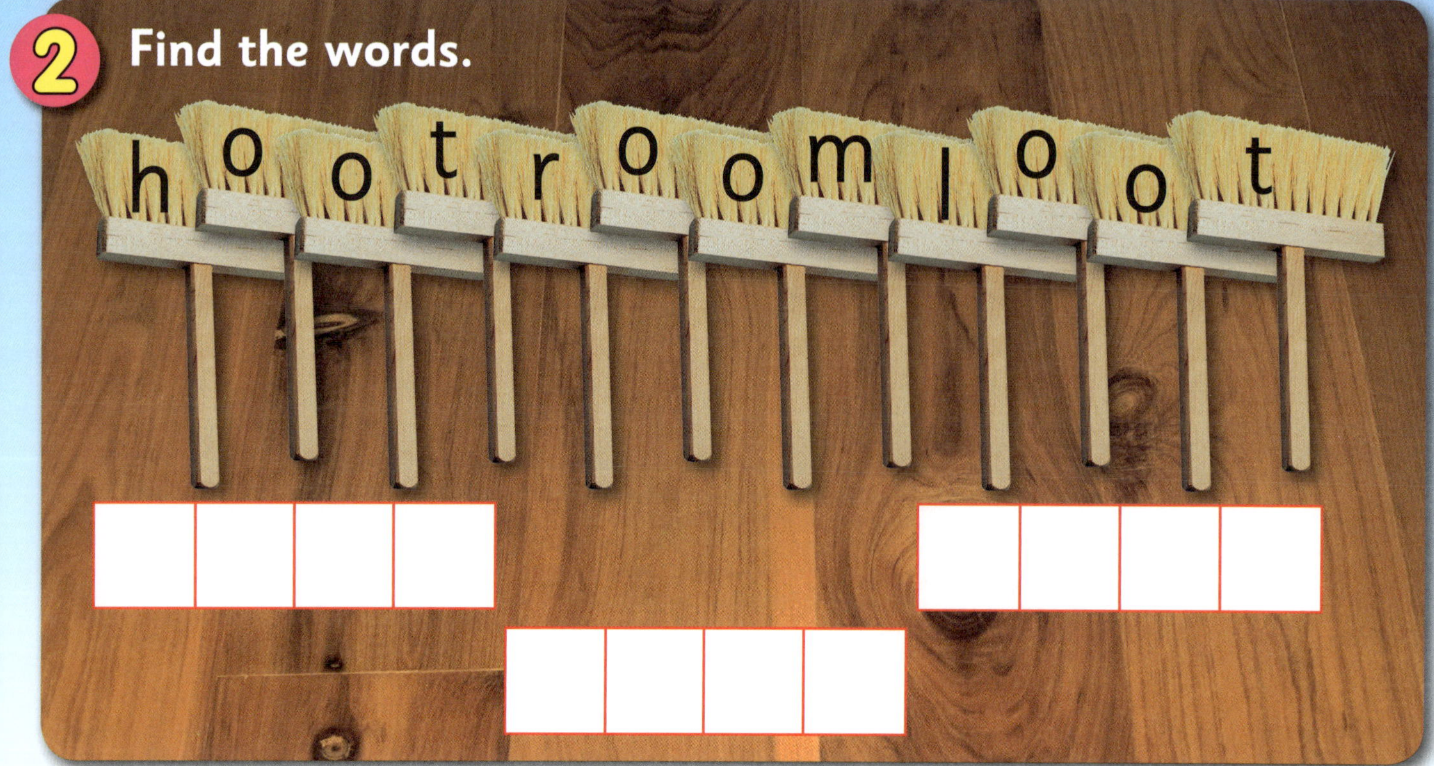

3 Complete the words. Use Bunky Boo's letters.

zoo___

shoo___

___ff

___ere

c___lled

4 Write a sentence using Red Rooster's word.

____

____

____

____

____

____

CHALLENGE Unjumble these words.

rhee _______________ thoso _______________

Lesson 30 • ump

Wordlist bump jump dump pump hump lump thump saw help mark stump crumple

1 Join the jigsaw pieces to make words. Write them.

2 Colour the **ump** words. Write them.

saw hump

dump

thump help

mark

crumple jump

ump words

3 **Read the clue to write the word.**

You can find me on a camel.
I am a ____________.

Cut a tree down and you have me.
I am a ____________.

Ouch! You can do this to your head.

____

You can do this on a trampoline.

____

4 **Complete the sentences.**

dump jump saw

Kangako can ____________ up and down.

Dan ____________ Frogfish in the pool.

Gus can ____________ lots of rubbish.

CHALLENGE

Write a rhyming word from your list for each word.

park yelp paw clump

Lesson 31 • More than one

Wordlist plugs casks lumps ducks belts tents hoops does going see schools stacks

1 Add **s** to make a **plural**.

plug
duck
schools
belt
lump
hoop

______ ______ ______

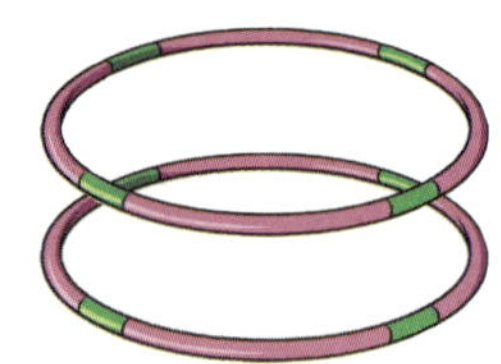

______ ______ ______

2 Colour the plural words.

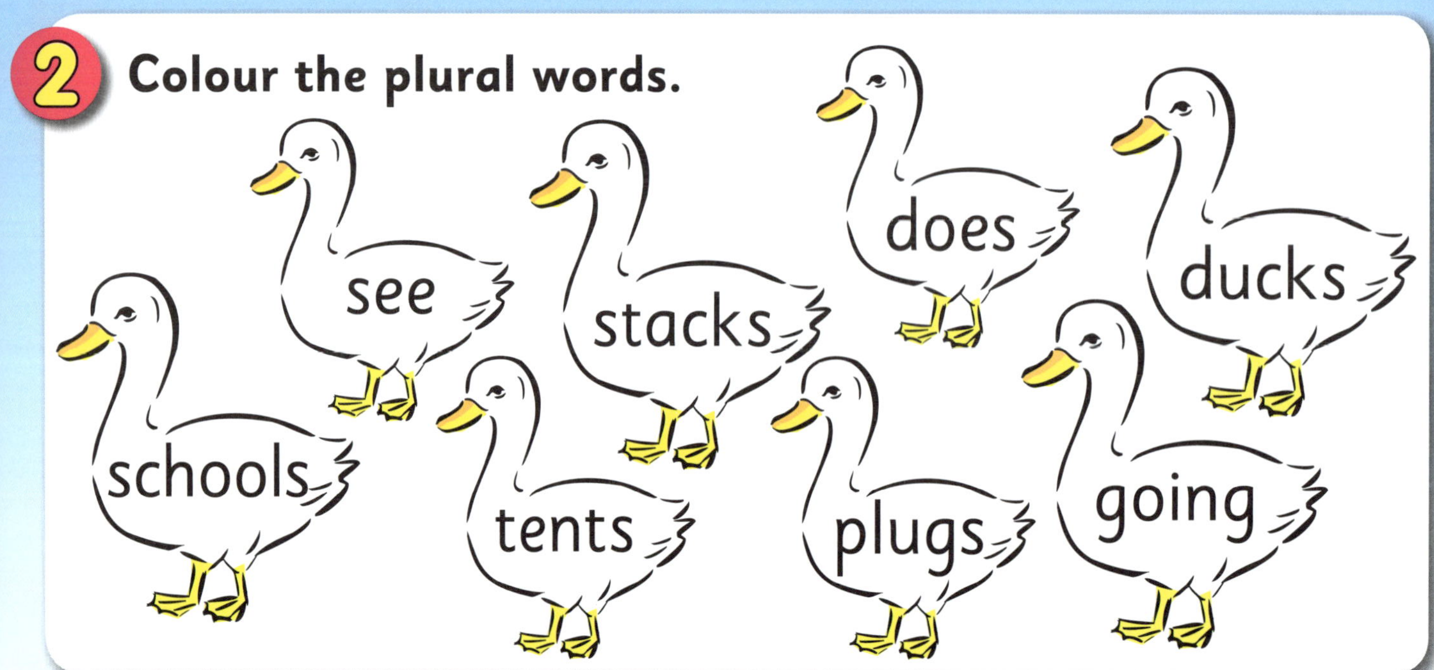

3 Follow the line. Write each word.

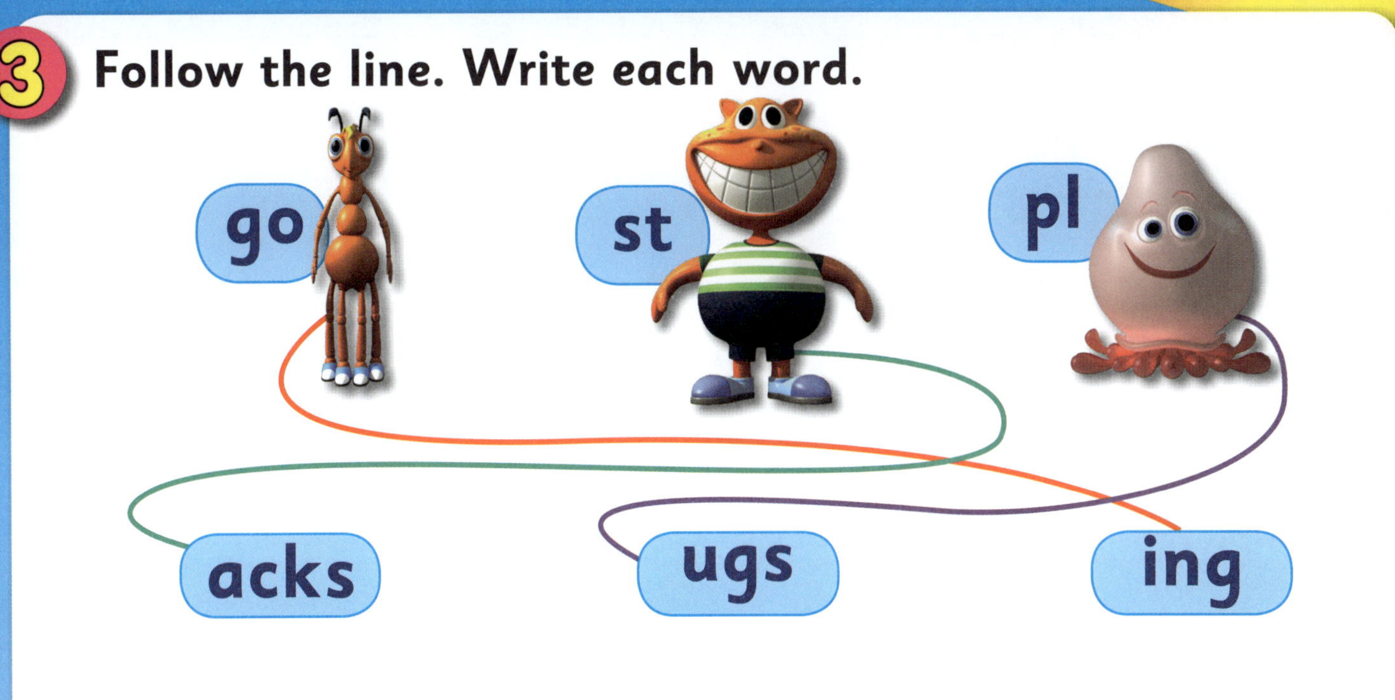

4 Complete the crossword.

1.

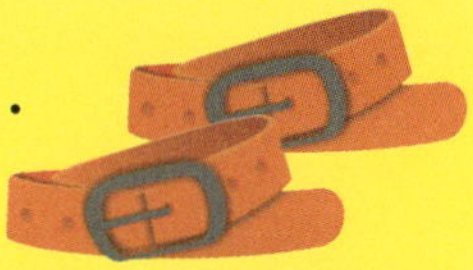

2.

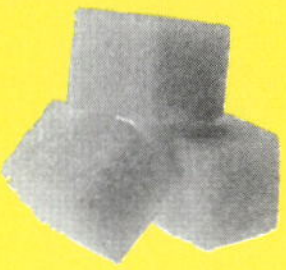

3.

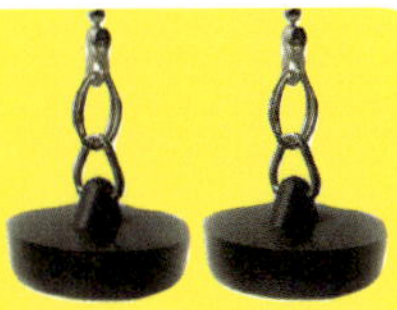

4.

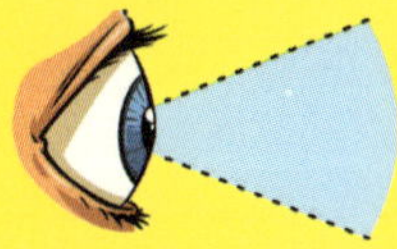

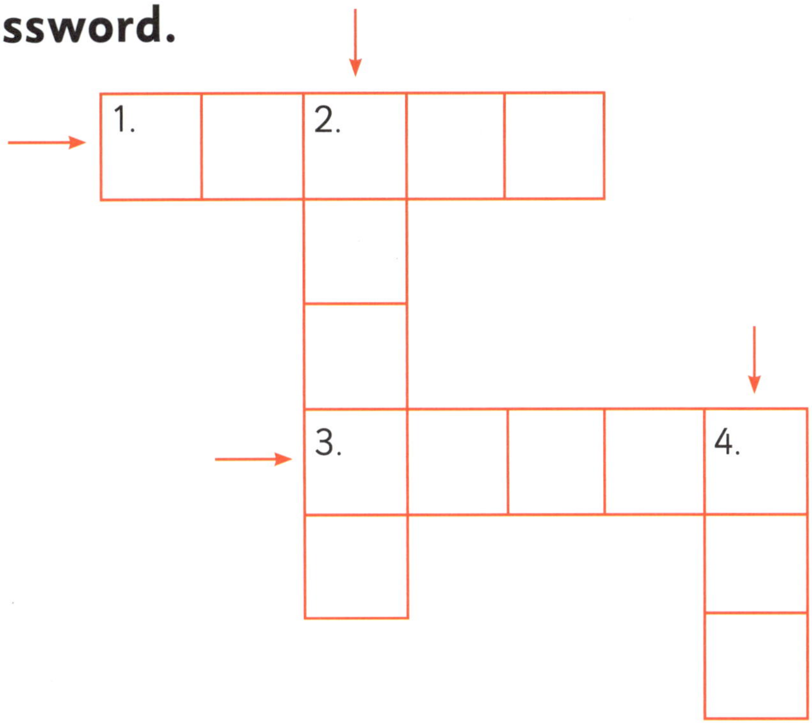

1.		2.					
		3.				4.	

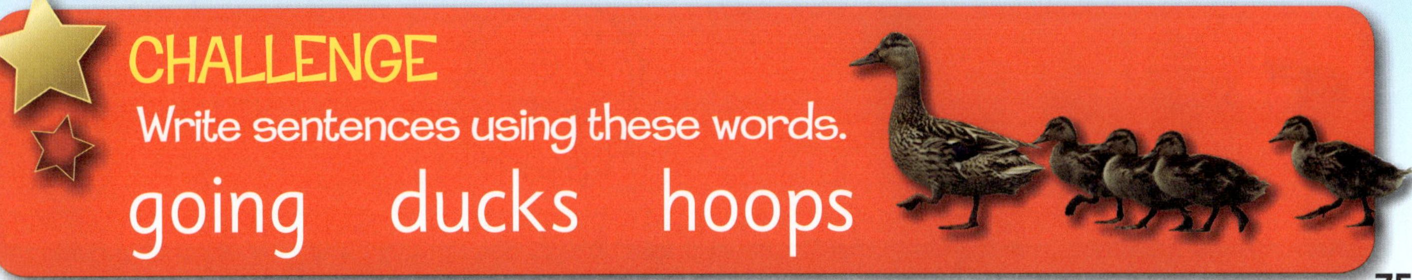

Lesson 32 • er

Wordlist helper hooter never father longer singer harder very children about summer mother

1 **Join each word to the er machine. Write each word you make.**

help long

hoot hard

2 **Label each picture.**

f

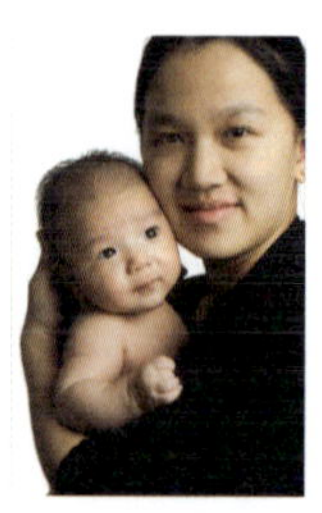

m

s

s

3 Trace and copy the words.

children ____________

summer ____________

4 Circle the correct word. Cross out the wrong word.

Me Be Fish is never nevver sad.

Lollipop Mop is verry very busy.

I know a story abowt about Sam.

CHALLENGE Circle the hidden words.

emotherfhsingertwnever

1 Complete the crossword. Use the picture clues to help you.

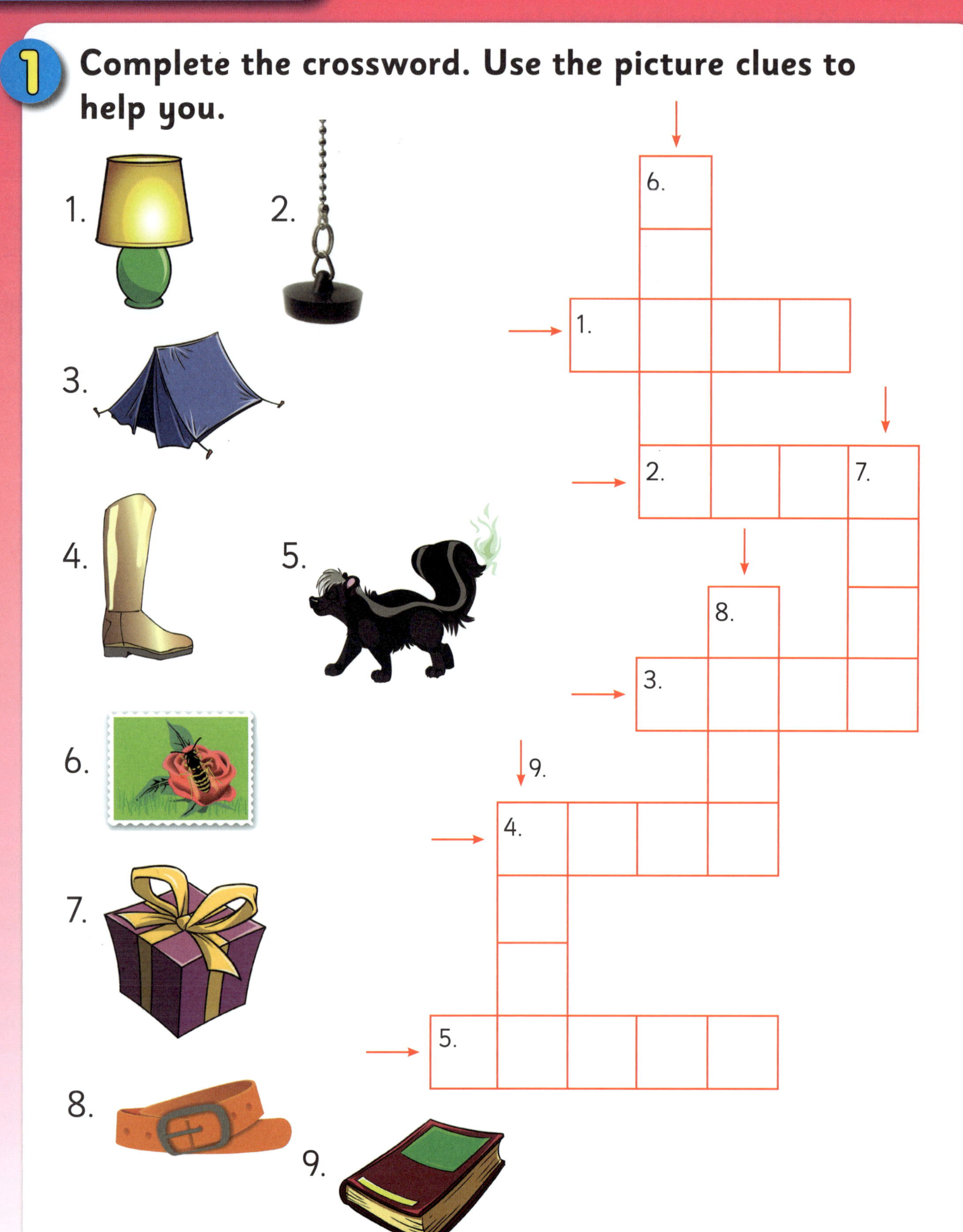

2 Power words. Join the letters to make the word.

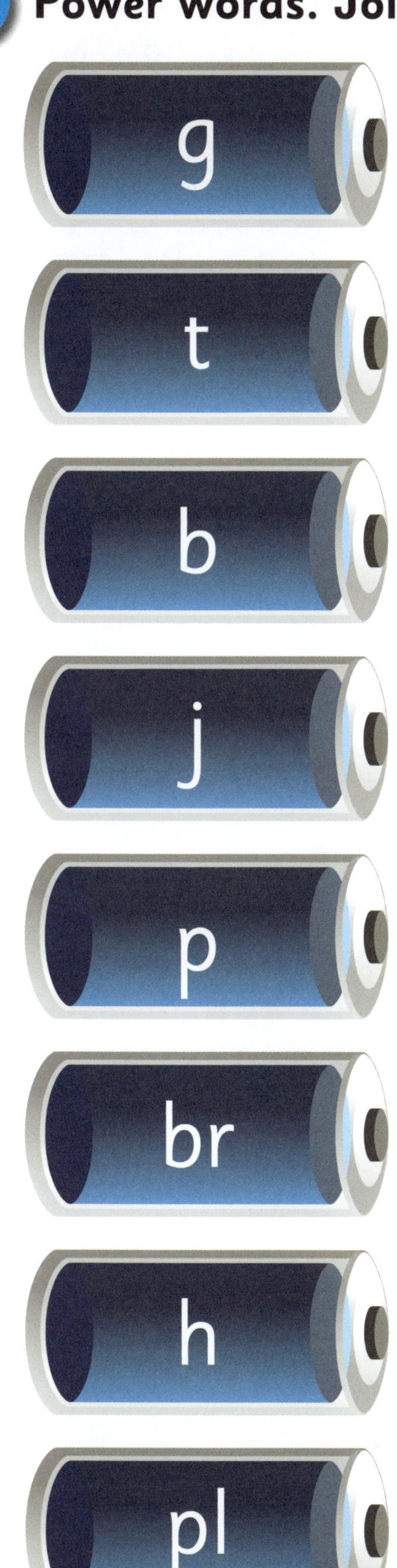

ABC
Reading
eggs
That's amazing!
knows how
to spell!